LOST LINERS

LOST LINERS

BY ROBERT D. BALLARD
and RICK ARCHBOLD
PAINTINGS BY KEN MARSCHALL

HISTORICAL CONSULTATION BY ERIC SAUDER

A HYPERION / MADISON PRESS BOOK

First published in the United States in 1997 by
Hyperion
114 Fifth Avenue
New York, N.Y. 10011
First paperback edition 1998.
Library of Congress Cataloging-in-Publication Data

Ballard, Robert D.
Lost liners: from the Titanic to the Andrea Doria the ocean
floor reveals its greatest lost ships/by Robert D. Ballard and
Rick Archbold; illustrations by Ken Marschall. — 1st ed.
        p. cm.
"A Hyperion/Madison Press Book."
Includes bibliographical references and index.

ISBN 0-7868-8384-7
1. Shipwrecks. 2. Ocean liners. I. Archbold, Rick II. Title.
G525.B256 1998
910.4'52 — dc21
97-15270
CIP

Produced by
Madison Press Books
40 Madison Avenue
Toronto, Ontario, Canada
M5R 2S1

Printed in Italy

To my son
William Benjamin Aymar Ballard

— *Robert D. Ballard*

To Walter Lord,
and all those who have brought
lost liners back to life

— *Rick Archbold*

For Rick Parks,
whose art was my inspiration

— *Ken Marschall*

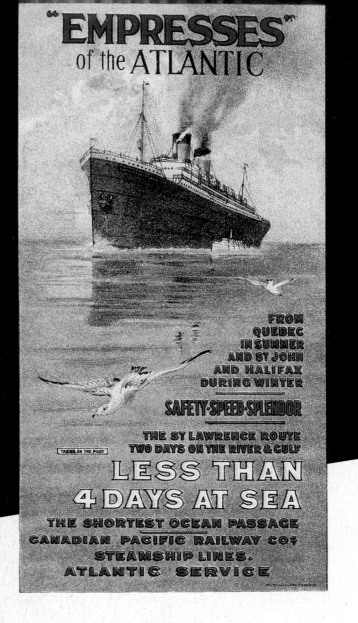

"EMPRESSES" of the ATLANTIC

FROM
QUEBEC
IN SUMMER
AND ST JOHN
AND HALIFAX
DURING WINTER

SAFETY·SPEED·SPLENDOR

THE ST LAWRENCE ROUTE
TWO DAYS ON THE RIVER & GULF

LESS THAN 4 DAYS AT SEA

THE SHORTEST OCEAN PASSAGE
CANADIAN PACIFIC RAILWAY CO$
STEAMSHIP LINES.
ATLANTIC SERVICE

"NORMANDIE"
THE WORLD'S MOST PERFECT SHIP

French Line

ENQUIRE WITHIN

IRISHM
AVENGE THE

JOIN AN IRIS
TO

ISSUED BY THE CENTRAL COUNCIL FOR THE ORGANISATION OF RECRUITING

Andrea Doria

Page 1: *Detail from a Norddeutscher
Lloyd Line advertisement of the 1920s.*
Pages 2-3: *The ill-fated Lusitania begins
its final plunge in May 1915.*
Pages 4-5: *The Royal Mail Steamer
Titanic begins her maiden voyage to
New York in April 1912.*
Pages 6-7: *The wreck of the Lusitania
is explored by the mini-submarine Delta
during our 1993 expedition.*
This page: *Colorful reminders of a
bygone era — posters advertising some
of history's greatest lost liners.*

Contents

Revisiting Lost Liners

The small crowd in the dining saloon aboard the *Carolyn Chouest* applauded and cheered as I cut into the anniversary cake, which the ship's chef had decorated with quite a passable rendering of the Royal Mail Steamer *Titanic* driving through choppy seas. Exactly ten years earlier, we had found the most famous of all shipwrecks, an event that had launched for me a decade of underwater exploration and discovery. Now I was floating under sunny skies in the calm Aegean roughly four hundred feet above the wreck of the *Titanic*'s younger sister, His Majesty's Hospital Ship *Britannic*. Back in September 1985, I'd been at my wit's end after a long and fruitless search for the *Titanic* in the bleak North Atlantic.

The memories came flooding back—the first gray images taken by ARGO, our deep-towed camera, of unidentifiable wreckage, then, bull's-eye, a boiler that unquestionably belonged to the *Titanic*. In the control van, pandemonium, jubilation—then the sudden realization that we had found the grave of fifteen hundred people. It was only many weeks later, back on land, as we pieced the wreck together from thousands of underwater snapshots, that the true state of the *Titanic* slowly emerged from the submarine gloom two and a half miles down. The bow was in amazingly good shape, the stern a blasted wasteland. I was determined to go back, to see the great ship up close.

The following summer, when we explored the wreck in our tiny submarine, *Alvin*, a dream came true for me and for countless *Titanic* buffs. I have written and spoken

Above: *Our 1995 research vessel, Carolyn Chouest, rides the calm Aegean just off the island of Kea.* Left: *Inside our research submarine, NR-1, I examine the wreck of the Britannic four hundred feet below.*

often of my first look at the ship, her proud bow parting the bottom mud as if it were an Atlantic swell—it's a mental image that will never fade. And the wonderful photographs from that expedition in the summer of 1986 seemed like the perfect grand tour. We had brought the ship back to light, but, except to land *Alvin* gently on her still-solid subdeck, we'd barely touched it, unless by accident. I had reason to hope that others would follow our lead. But it was not to be.

Through the *Titanic*, I had become acquainted with the fabulous heyday of ocean travel, and she had led me to other great wrecks, including the one that lay below me now. I'd been terrified that the *Britannic* would be as treacherous as the *Lusitania* had been when we'd explored her two years before. On the ruined hulk of the great Cunarder, we'd encountered fiendish currents, poor visibility, unexploded depth charges and, worst of all, a seemingly endless maze of snagged fishing nets. But so far the *Britannic* had turned out to be almost the perfect wreck, the friendliest I'd ever been on. She was the spitting image of the *Titanic*, but splendidly whole, amazingly well preserved.

Except for the forwardmost part of her bow, distorted badly by the impact with the bottom, *Britannic* was all there, in one magnificent piece, lying on her side. Exploring her intact stern had been the highlight of our expedition so far. Here, amazingly, was the missing half of the torn *Titanic* picture I'd been holding for ten years in my mind's eye. Now I could piece the picture together in my imagination. I could see the *Titanic* whole again.

But the wreck of the *Britannic* had her own story to tell, and in the next few days we hoped to unravel it. There was something demure about this wreck; it reminded me of a bride in her wedding dress who never quite made it to the altar. Certainly the image of the never-wed bride fits her life story. World War I diverted the *Britannic*— the last of White Star's three giant sisters to be launched—from her intended career as a great passenger liner to serving her country as a hospital ship. That's why she was wearing white the day she went down, steaming innocently toward the Aegean island of Lemnos to retrieve wounded soldiers from the Mediterranean theater. No rich or famous patrons would ever paddle in her pool, take tea in her Verandah Café or dine in the Ritz-inspired intimacy of her à la carte restaurant. Her brief life was a promise unfulfilled, a vow never exchanged.

Aboard the *Carolyn Chouest*, our brief *Titanic* anniversary celebration dwindled to a close as the assembled team members drifted back to their tasks. Artist Ken Marschall, barely able to contain his excitement, had thoughts only for his first trip to the *Britannic* wreck in *NR-1*, the navy's pint-sized nuclear-powered submarine we had borrowed for our *Britannic* mission. Then historian Eric Sauder would take his turn. But for the duration of our time on site, I would direct the proceedings from our control van, quarterbacking our two remotely operated robot vehicles, *Phantom* and *Voyager*, from the solid deck of the support ship, delighting in the images they'd capture but no

Top: Voyager, *one of our two remotely controlled camera vehicles, is launched over the side of the ship.*
Above: *The control panel of* NR-1.

Top: *The submarine NR-1 runs on the surface.*
Above: *The elaborate marine encrustations on the* Britannic *wreck reminded me of the decorations on a wedding cake.*

longer feeling the need to spend long, uncomfortable hours in a cramped submarine. No, exploring the site via video camera—what I call telepresence—is better.

My dream for the *Britannic* wreck is permanent telepresence. Now that I see just how good the wreck's condition is, I can already envisage the world's first underwater museum. There would be a visitors' center on the nearby island of Kea, linked to the wreck by a fiberoptic cable. Cameras mounted on tracks could travel along the hull and venture inside the ship. Given how well preserved the wreck is, I'd bet some of the interior spaces are remarkably intact. And we could use modern preservation techniques to arrest the process of decay so that our submarine exhibits would operate indefinitely. But first, the Greek government and the wreck's current owner would have to agree.

If this dream ever comes true, it will stand in stark contrast to the sad story of the *Titanic* wreck in the ten years since our discovery. Those who insist on salvage miss the magic and the mystery of these great wrecks, which remind me of famous battlefields preserved exactly as they were the moment the battle ended. If we can visit them and explore them at our will, then why dismantle them and put them in museum displays detached from their context and missing a lot of their meaning?

The great age of the ocean liner is gone. Apart from the *Queen Mary*, now a soulless dockside hotel, almost all the fabulous ships have been broken up and sold as scrap, their interior fittings auctioned off to collectors. Ironically, however, the truly "lost" liners that sank at sea form the real legacy of this vanished age. I have been privileged to visit five of them, the *Titanic*, the *Britannic*, the *Lusitania*, the *Andrea Doria* and the *Republic*, which sank off Nantucket in 1909. The sea has preserved them for us in various stages of destruction and decay, but they are all still recognizably themselves and incomparably more impressive than if they were on display in some drydock Disneyland.

On this sunny September day in the Aegean, as I headed back to the control van and the video images of the *Britannic* wreck, I was suddenly aware that these past ten years had brought me into close contact with great ships that span the fifty-year heyday of the transatlantic superliner from the *Lusitania* to the *Andrea Doria*. These lost liners have been found. And they evoke a magnificent epic of triumph and tragedy.

Chapter

1

In 1819 an American ship
made the first steam-assisted
crossing of the Atlantic. But it was
not until the birth of the Cunard
Line in 1840 that a steamship
company could promise to deliver
its passengers to their destinations
on a regular schedule. And it would
be many more years before metal-
hulled giants had completely
replaced their sailing rivals, able to
offer not only reliability and safety,
but luxury—and even comfort.

*A romanticized vision of the Great Eastern of 1860,
a ship so far ahead of her time that no vessel matched
her size until the turn of the century.*

A Better Way to Cross

The Birth of the Transatlantic Ocean Liner, 1819 ~ 1900

I n January 1842, the thirty-year-old Charles Dickens, his wife, Kate, and their maid took passage from Liverpool to Boston on the *Britannia*, one of the four Cunard steamers then plying the North Atlantic between Britain and America. The already-famous English novelist had been invited to the New World for a series of lectures and dramatic readings from his hugely popular works, *The Pickwick Papers* and *Nicholas Nickleby*. It is unlikely he would have made the trip for pleasure. The era of true liner luxury was still many years away.

The North Atlantic is one of the roughest oceans in the world and in winter is at its most inhospitable—as Dickens and his wife soon discovered. Their stormy voyage became a melancholy endurance marathon. Dickens spent many days in a seasick semicoma in a claustrophobic stateroom that had struck him on his boarding the ship as an "utterly impractical, thoroughly hopeless and profoundly preposterous box," his discomfort made worse by the lack of ventilation and the pervasive "compound of strange smells, which is to be found nowhere but on board ship, and which is such a subtle perfume that it seems to enter at every pore of the skin, and whisper of the hold." What was subtle to a nineteenth-century nose would almost certainly seem intolerable to a twentieth-century one. This typical mid-nineteenth-century passenger ship had no heating system, no running water, no toilets and no way of keeping food fresh once the ice had melted. A cow kept on deck provided a limited supply of fresh milk.

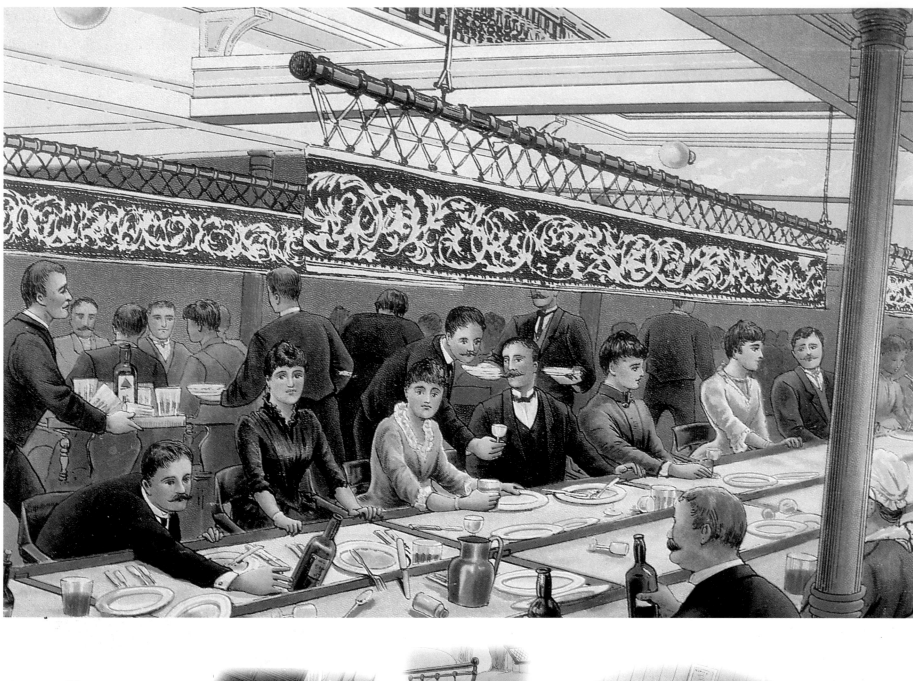

When the weather finally relented and Dickens and his fellow passengers gained their sea legs and recovered their appetites, they gathered daily in the ship's "grand" saloon, which the author likened to a "hearse with windows." This space doubled as lounge and dining room, the food being brought below from the cookhouse on deck—in bad weather, it often arrived cold and occasionally seasoned with salt water. The *Britannia*'s passengers ate heartily and took "as long as possible about it," although the monotonous fare of meat and potatoes declined in quality as the voyage stretched into its third week. After "a rather moldy dessert of apples, grapes and oranges," the men drank brandy and played whist at the saloon table, in rough weather placing the cards in their pockets to keep them from sliding onto the floor.

Eighteen days after leaving England, and after a brief stop in Halifax, the *Britannia* finally reached Boston. "The indescribable interest with which I strained my eyes, as the first patches of American soil peeped like molehills from the green sea, and followed them, as they swelled, by slow and almost imperceptible degrees, into a continuous line of coast, can hardly be exaggerated," Dickens wrote. And, despite the fierce midwinter cold, he did not leave the rail until the ship was safely moored to the wharf.

Dickens's famous account of his journey colored the reputation of transatlantic travel for many years, long after the conditions he described had given way to considerably greater comfort. But it does seem to accurately evoke shipboard life at a time when the ocean steamship was still in its infancy and when passage by sailing packet, though less reliable, was usually considerably more comfortable.

Cunard's first four small steamers, all commissioned in 1840-41, had actually launched something completely new in ocean travel: regular, reliable service on a fixed departure schedule. No one knew it then, but this pioneering company would outlast all its rivals and, in the process, establish an unmatched safety record. The tone was set

Previous page: A painting showing a deck scene on a steamer of the 1880s.
Opposite: Although staterooms on the early steamships were tiny, dressing for dinner was de rigeur. But even the most privileged passengers ate boarding-house style at long tables. Eventually the padded benches of the early steamers gave way to individual armchairs, albeit still bolted firmly to the floor.
Above: Conditions in steerage were often atrocious and serious diseases, such as cholera, could decimate the third-class passenger list.
Right: Samuel Cunard of Halifax, the visionary founder of the Cunard Steamship Line, which survives to the present day.

by the operating instructions laid down by the company's founder, Samuel Cunard of Halifax, to his very first captain: "It will be very obvious to you that it is of the first importance to the Partners of the *Britannia* that she attains the Character for Speed and Safety." Safety would continue to be the firm's watchword. Later in the century, an admiring Mark Twain would opine, "The Cunard people would not take Noah himself as first mate till they had worked him through all the lower grades and tried him ten years or such matter."

However, reliability was rare in those pioneering days, and nautical technology would need many long years of development before steam completely displaced sail. The nineteenth century saw great waves of emigration from the Old World to the New, but in the early days of steam, few emigrants arrived under power. The four original Cunard ships, each with space for only 115 passengers, made no provision for steerage passengers at all, concentrating on their main task, which was the speedy and safe delivery of the Royal Mail.

Above: An Arctic chill in January 1844 froze Boston Harbor and trapped Britannia, threatening Cunard's reputation for reliability. But some of Boston's leading citizens put up the money to cut an ice channel through which the ship made a daring escape.
Opposite top left: A Cunard passenger list from the Pavonia.
Opposite top right: The Savannah, which made the first steam-assisted Atlantic crossing in 1819.
Opposite bottom left: A Cunard sailing schedule from the 1850s.

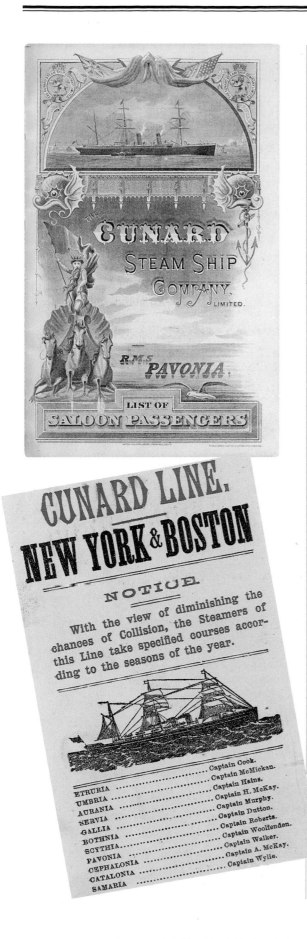

For many years, they would continue to do so with a strong assist from wind power. These early steamers weren't pure steamships at all, but wooden-hulled hybrids, sailing ships with steam engines and great side paddle wheels. They used their sails whenever possible, both to enhance speed and to promote fuel economy. Coal was bulky and expensive, and making steam was a noisy and dirty process. In fact, several pioneering steamships gave up their engines and reverted to the sailing life after failing to live up to their builders' promises.

Such false starts were hardly surprising, given the then brief history of the steamer at sea. Marine historians enjoy debating the pivotal moments in the early story of this developing technology, but the incontrovertible facts are these. In 1819, the *Savannah*, an American sailing ship with auxiliary steam engines and two paddle wheels that could be folded away on deck, made the first steam-assisted crossing of the Atlantic. In reality, she used her engines only a fraction of the time and mostly when she was in sight of critical eyes ashore. Not until 1831, did a ship—the Canadian paddle steamer *Royal*

William—finally cross the Atlantic primarily under steam, although she needed to stop her engines every few days for twenty-four hours to scrape the accumulated salt deposits from her boilers. During those times, she depended entirely on her sails. Finally, in 1838, the *Sirius*, a new coastal steamer temporarily commandeered for a transocean voyage, became the first ship to cross the Atlantic under continuous steam power.

By the late 1830s—before Cunard even entered the picture—three separate British companies were vying to be the first to inaugurate regular transatlantic steamship travel. But only one of their initial ships made any lasting impression. This was the *Great Western*, brainchild of Isambard Kingdom Brunel, already one of Britain's most successful civil engineers. The ship was owned by Britain's Great Western Railway, and her builders envisaged her as an ocean link with the railway's land-transportation network, a scheme eventually accomplished by the Canadian Pacific steamships of a later era.

When the *Great Western* made her maiden voyage from Bristol to New York in April 1838, she entirely lived up to her

Left: *The Great Western was the first and most successful of the pioneering steamships created by the brilliant Isambard Kingdom Brunel.*
Above: *Brunel poses in front of the chain cable soon to be used for launching the* Great Eastern.

advance billing. She was bigger and faster and more beautifully appointed than any ship before her. Her grand saloon was the grandest yet seen, with its Gothic-revival arches and elegant wall-panel paintings done in the delicate style of Watteau. Her passengers no longer had to emerge from their cabins to shout for a steward, but could summon him simply by pulling on a bell-rope. But where the *Great Western* truly stood out was in her performance. Over the subsequent eight years, she accomplished sixty-four round trips between Bristol and New York. Had her owners been able to build equally reliable sisters quickly, they could have given Cunard a run for his money. But not until 1845 did the

Great Eastern: A Ship Ahead of Her Time

Brunel's Great Britain, *here being launched at Bristol, was plagued with operational problems almost from her first voyage to New York in July of 1845.*

Great Western get a companion, the *Great Britain*. A fabulous ship, she was perhaps the first true ocean liner: she had an iron hull, watertight bulkheads, a double bottom and was the first transatlantic steamship to replace paddle wheels with screw propulsion. Although she was for many years the largest ship in the world, her performance never lived up to expectations. In only her second season, just when early problems with her power plant seemed solved, she ran aground off the Irish coast owing to an egregious navigational error. Although all 180 passengers made it safely ashore, the ship was only refloated the following spring, by which time her owners had gone bankrupt and were forced to sell her.

The four durable wooden-hulled Cunarders that all came into service within the space of a single year gave their company a virtual monopoly on the North Atlantic

Edward Knight Collins, founder of the Collins line.

during the pioneering decade of the 1840s. Not until 1851 did Cunard face its first serious rival. Then, for slightly more than ten years, a fleet of American passenger steamers temporarily took the lead. The competition between the Cunard Line and the Collins Line in the 1850s foreshadowed the ruthless battle for preeminence that would characterize the transatlantic passenger trade in the closing decades of the century.

Edward Knight Collins was already a successful operator of sailing packets when, in 1845, he applied to the U.S. Congress for a mail subsidy that would help him

No new ship has ever attempted a leap into the future as bold as the *Great Eastern*'s. Fifty years after she was launched—twenty years after she had been scrapped—she still held the record as the largest and longest ship ever built. In terms of construction and passenger accommodation she belonged to a later era.

The name *Great Eastern* symbolized the dream that led to her construction. She was to be the first steamship to make a regular passage between England and Australia, pausing for refueling only once — at Calcutta. In the mid-nineteenth century, the scarcity of ports capable of providing coal severely limited a ship's range. To reach India on one load of fuel, the *Great Eastern* required enormous storage capacity — this was the primary reason for her unprecedented size.

Almost from the start she seemed an ill-starred ship. Technical problems slowed her construction and put her disastrously over budget. When launch day finally came, ten thousand invited guests watched as the great hulk slid broadside down the ways, then stopped dead and refused to budge. It ultimately took more than a month and an additional £170,000 to get her into the water. By the time she

Above: *The Great Eastern dwarfed every other ship of her day.*
Right: *Brunel (in stovepipe hat) visits his "great babe" during construction.*
Far right: *The Great Eastern arrives in New York at the end of her maiden voyage.*
Left: *A conch shell decorated with an image of the Great Eastern.*

was finally afloat, the original owners teetered on the brink of bankruptcy.

But she remained an obsession for her designing engineer, Isambard Kingdom Brunel, who called her his "great babe" and continued to direct her completion under her new owners, who abandoned all thoughts of the Far East in favor of the transatlantic run. On her sea trials, a ruptured heater caused a violent explosion that launched the forward funnel like a rocket and badly scalded many of the stokehold crew. Four ultimately died. Then her first captain drowned in a boating mishap. Fortunately for Brunel's peace of mind, he died of a stroke before the *Great Eastern*'s maiden voyage.

After innumerable delays and much bad press, the *Great Eastern* left Liverpool on June 17, 1860, carrying only forty-six passengers, eight of them non-paying guests, in quarters designed to accommodate four thousand. Despite her great size she "rolled like a drowsy walrus" in bad weather and was never popular with passengers. Her one small claim to glory would be laying the first transatlantic cable.

In 1888, she was finally put out of her misery, but not out of memory. Never has a ship been so ahead of her time, or so out of step with it.

finance a fleet of vessels to challenge Cunard. (Samuel Cunard's success in securing the British mail subsidy had made his line viable, though seldom profitable.) In Collins's successful Dramatic Line of sailing packets, each named after a famous actor or playwright, he had demonstrated a flair for showmanship and a taste for lavishness that he would now use to good effect against the slightly stodgy, ever-safety-conscious Cunard.

In what would quickly become the reigning theme of the race for the North Atlantic, Collins's American-designed-and-built ships were bigger (more than twice as large as their Cunard rivals), more powerful and more luxurious than almost anything seen before. No longer would one room serve as both lounge and dining saloon. On Collins's first ship, the *Atlantic* of 1850, there was a drawing room and a separate dining room, lined with mirrors, paneled in expensive wood and richly furnished. Even more innovative, there were bathrooms, a barber shop and the first-ever smoking room—actually a cramped little deckhouse, but a hint of grander things to come. The public rooms were steam heated and the ice room held forty tons of ice, enough to

Above: *The Collins steamer* Atlantic *and her sisters set a new standard for shipboard luxury.* Below: *The* Atlantic's *drawing room boasted plush chairs and sofas and tabletops of Brocatelli marble.*

Above: *In 1865, during the* Great Eastern's *first attempt at laying a transatlantic cable, the cable repeatedly broke, requiring frequent splicing, and was ultimately lost. The next year, however, the operation was successfully completed.*
Above far left: *Two of the ship's interiors, photographed by the renowned Montreal photographer William Notman.*
Left: *In a final ignominy, the* Great Eastern *ended her days as a floating billboard off Liverpool.*

keep food fresh for the duration of a voyage. But the "staterooms" remained small, cramped and double occupancy. True comfort, as opposed to the trappings of luxury, had yet to be realized.

Staterooms notwithstanding, the Collins Line quickly established records for speed and a reputation for glamour that made its ships the preferred choice for the passenger trade. On her return voyage from Liverpool, the *Atlantic* broke the previous speed record; the *Pacific* became the first ship to cross the Atlantic in fewer than ten days.

Faced with such superior competition, Cunard might well have become a historical footnote were it not for the unfortunate tendency of Collins liners to get into serious seafaring trouble. The *Atlantic*'s maiden voyage to England in the spring of 1850 was dogged by mishaps, beginning on the first day out of New York when drift ice damaged her paddle wheels. Then she had engine trouble. But at least she limped safely into Liverpool harbor. Two of her sisters would not be so lucky.

In September 1854 the *Arctic*, which happened to be carrying Collins's wife and two of his children, was rammed by a smaller, but iron-hulled, French steamer in fog off the Grand Banks. The Frenchman lost his bow but managed to limp safely into St. John's, Newfoundland. The *Arctic* sank before the captain could beach her. Three hundred and forty-six people drowned, including all three Collinses along with five members of the family of Collins's partner, James Brown. Only two years later, the *Pacific* vanished during a January passage to Liverpool and no trace of her turned up until 1986, when a fisherman snagged his nets on a shipwreck in the Irish Sea between Anglesea and the Isle of Man.

During this same month, Cunard's first iron ship, *Persia*, ran smack into an iceberg but managed to stay afloat and safely finish the voyage to New York. The loss of the *Pacific*, combined with the successful escape of the *Persia*, finished off Collins's reputation and refurbished Cunard's. By the early 1860s, the Collins Line had folded. But Cunard was facing a whole new breed of competition, all of it British. Soon these rivals included the Oceanic Steam Navigation Company, or White Star Line, founded in 1869 by Thomas Ismay.

For the final four decades of the nineteenth century, Great Britain virtually owned the North Atlantic. Year after year, ships wearing the red ensign of the British merchant marine captured the coveted Blue Riband, the mythical trophy for the fastest transatlantic passage. The Liverpool-New York run, a trip that almost never took less than ten days in 1856, was regularly accomplished in fewer than six by the 1890s. With the Industrial Revolution at its frantic zenith, important technological advances appeared with inexorable frequency as steamships assumed a recognizably modern shape. Wooden hulls gave way to iron, then iron to stronger and more workable steel, permitting ever-larger ships with vaster passenger spaces. Simple engines became more

The Collins Line foundered on its abysmal safety record.
Top: *The Arctic, which sank in September 1854 with great loss of life, including Collins's wife and two of his children.*
Above: *Chaos reigns on deck as the Arctic sinks.*

WRECK OF THE U.S.M.STEAM SHIP "ARCTIC".

OFF CAPE RACE WEDNESDAY SEPTEMBER 27TH 1854.

Above: Panicked crewmen occupied all but one of the Arctic's lifeboats, accounting for the heavy loss of life among the passengers.

efficient (and more powerful) compound engines, as one stack became two and then three, emblems to the seagoing public of both size and power. The paddle wheel died a long-overdue death, replaced by the single screw and then twin screws, whose reliability finally made sails unnecessary. Even if one propeller was dropped, the ship could continue its journey. Steamers still carried sails until late in the century, but these gradually dwindled until all that remained were flag masts.

Without a rapidly rising demand for a fast and safe Atlantic passage, however, these great advances would have come much more slowly. The late nineteenth century was an age of mass migration from Great Britain and Europe to the New World and it was the steerage, or third-class, passenger who provided the basic income that allowed the proliferating steamship lines to thrive. Steerage passengers paid low fares, and they received very little in return in terms of shipboard comfort, but steamers offered a considerable improvement over the "coffin brigs" of the eighteenth century, on which filthy conditions, poor ventilation and lack of food led to shipboard epidemics and a heavy death toll. The first company to seize the emigration opportunity was the Liverpool-based Inman Line, which began by specializing in the steerage trade, but Cunard, White Star and others soon made the adjustment, increasing their steerage capacity and improving its amenities.

Yet what most vividly marks this period of rapid passenger steamship evolution is the ascending star of luxury. If a company's bread and butter came from the steerage trade, glamour and prestige came not just from speed but also from a ship's first-class image. Each new ship that joined the North Atlantic run seemed to boast a higher standard of luxe and comfort. The privileged personages who increasingly walked the promenade decks or whiled away shipboard hours in plush lounges and clubby smoking rooms provided an aura of romance for what was, in truth, a rather cut-throat business. For the wealthy traveler, these ships offered ever-grander and more decorative public rooms, finer food and more spacious staterooms with the most modern conveniences—including private bathrooms with hot and cold running water, electric light and steam heat.

In the evolution of liner luxe, there is no clear moment when passenger steamships became fancy floating hotels—at least in first class—but by the turn of the century, this transition had been clearly and irrevocably accomplished. Increasing size meant more and more space for designers to create the illusion that the traveler had never left dry land.

The new White Star Line's maiden liner *Oceanic*, commissioned in 1871, was the first to move first-class quarters away from the stern—relatively high and dry in the days of sail but prone to uncomfortable propeller vibrations in steamships—to the middle of

The Evolution of the Atlantic Liner

In the early days, Atlantic steamships looked more like their sailing forebears than their sleeker descendants. Even the earliest screw-propelled steamers, such as Cunard's Cuba of the 1860s, supplemented steam with windpower whenever possible. But during the closing decades of the nineteenth century, as wood gave way to iron and iron to steel, the ships carrying passengers between Europe and the New World rapidly assumed a more modern appearance.

Cunard's Batavia of 1870 still sports a clipperlike bowsprit and has sailing masts that tower over one small funnel.

White Star's Celtic of 1872, though only two years younger than Batavia, has the blunt bow of later liners, but is prepared to hoist sails when possible.

Cunard's Servia of 1881 shows that by the 1880s passenger steamships had virtually left their sailing days behind.

the ship, and the first to open up the dining saloon to occupy a vessel's full width. In this ample space, where coal-burning fireplaces with marble mantels gave the illusion of a grand country house, passengers for the first time sat down to dinner in separate armchairs, albeit ones bolted to the floor, rather than the long padded benches of yore.

The National Line's *America* of 1884 not only claimed the first Blue Riband speed record for a steel-hulled ship but also boasted the first glass dome over a dining saloon. The I & I Line's *City of New York* (1888) and *City of Paris* (1889) not only were the first twin-screwed liners on the North Atlantic run but also introduced a handful of dining alcoves as more intimate alternatives to the long refectory-style tables where most of the passengers still took their meals. The builders also provided fourteen private suites comprising a bedroom and sitting room that could have been lifted from a contemporary Victorian house. According to one observer, on these two ships, "Luxury has been carried just as far as the present human invention and imagination can take it."

Through the 1890s the trend continued, but as yet no single aesthetic sensibility had imposed order and restraint on what had become an orgy of overstuffed, overdecorated late-Victorian eclecticism. This couldn't last. More and more wealthy Americans made

Above and below: *The City of New York, the first twin-screwed liner on the Atlantic run, awed its passengers with a glass-domed dining room with seats for 420 and a walnut-paneled smoking room accommodating 130. It also had an 800-volume library, with a floor plan shaped like an hourglass, embellished with stained-glass windows bearing evocative fragments of nautical poesy.*

Top and below: The most distinguished visitor aboard the new White Star liner Teutonic *during the naval review at Spithead in August 1889 was Kaiser Wilhelm II. The kaiser was so impressed with the ship and its amenities, which included a barber shop with electrically driven hairdrying fans, that he famously remarked, "We must have some of these."*

Above right: By the time the Kaiser Wilhelm der Grosse *entered service a decade later, Germany had displaced Great Britain as the preeminent passenger-carrying nation.*

the annual pilgrimage to London and the Continent as part of their regular social season, and they were gaining knowledge and taste that outstripped conservative British fashions. It was only a matter of time before the country-house luxury of the British evolved into a more sophisticated, more European *grand luxe*. The purveyors of this sea change turned out to be Britain's only real rivals on the Atlantic scene, the Germans.

To say that the Germans invented the twentieth-century luxury liner might be overstating the case, but they surely combined the existing strands of liner evolution to bring it into being. In the late 1890s their ships rapidly overtook the British in terms of size and speed. Norddeutscher Lloyd's *Kaiser Wilhelm der Grosse* of 1897, the pioneering four-stacker, was the first non-British ship to hold the Blue Riband since the demise of the Collins Line. And Hamburg-Amerika's *Deutschland* of 1900, despite excessive vibration and an appetite for coal that made her a perennial money loser, would take the Atlantic speed record on her maiden voyage and hold it for six years.

But these two aggressive German companies, themselves fierce rivals, left a greater imprint on shipboard style than on marine engineering. They were the first to turn over the artistic control for designing a passenger liner's interiors to a single architect/designer.

In the case of Lloyd's *Kaiser Wilhelm der Grosse* and her three subsequent sisters, the organizing genius was a gentleman from Bremen by the name of Johannes Poppe.

Schooled in the beaux-arts tradition, with a strong preference for baroque revival, Poppe should have had the middle name Grandiosity. Historian John Malcolm Brinnin describes the *Kaiser Wilhelm der Grosse* as "a sea-going boast," whose public rooms, with their impossibly high ceilings, ornate carvings and bas-reliefs, their gilt-

Albert Ballin.

framed mirrors and glowing stained glass, represented an "outsized magnificence." "Instead of quietly charming the well-to-do passenger by reminding him of his home, his club, or a familiar country inn," Brinnin writes, "the new designers overwhelmed and overawed him." Poppe's grand designs would undoubtedly offend our present-day sensibilities, but, at the turn of the century, they made the new Lloyd ships the most fashionable on the North Atlantic run.

It fell to Hamburg-Amerika (HAPAG), however, to temper Poppe's palatial grandeur with a more restrained aesthetic and truly to set the tone for the great ships to come. After the *Deutschland*'s disappointing performance, HAPAG's managing director, Albert Ballin, decreed that comfort and luxury, not speed, would be his watchwords. Ballin, whose ferocious work habits and obsessive eye for detail had made his company the biggest single Atlantic carrier by the turn of the century, soon found the perfect person to carry out his new intentions.

Top, above and below: *Hamburg-Amerika's* Deutschland *of 1900, which was fast but uncomfortable and plagued with operating problems, convinced Albert Ballin to focus on grand luxe and creature comforts rather than speed. In 1910 she was removed from service to be transformed into a cruising liner renamed* Viktoria Luise.

The first examples of Ballin's new operating philosophy were the Amerika *of 1905 (below) and the* Kaiserin Auguste Viktoria *of 1906 (bottom), the first ships to offer first-class passengers a stylish à la carte restaurant modeled after the fashionable Ritz-Carlton Grill in London—and with food to match. The latter ship was originally to be christened* Europa, *but it proved more politic to name her after the kaiser's consort.*

On one of Ballin's periodic stopovers in London—he had been visiting the shipbuilders Harland & Wolff in Belfast to check on the progress of a new ship—he paused to dine at the Carlton Hotel's new Ritz-Carlton Grill. Here he encountered not only the lavish haute cuisine of Auguste Escoffier but also the tasteful interiors of a French architect named Charles Mewès. Ballin was so smitten by the combination that he determined his next ship would contain a floating version of the Ritz-Carlton Grill, an à la carte alternative—at an additional price—to the first-class dining room. Here was a golden carrot to attract the cream of the Edwardian *beau monde*. He sought out Mewès and offered him the commission to design the interiors of the *Amerika*. Then he approached César Ritz and asked him to oversee the restaurant. The two Frenchmen accepted, and a fruitful, enduring partnership was born.

Mewès's *Amerika* became a floating grand hotel par excellence. So popular was her Ritz-Carlton Restaurant on the ship's maiden voyage in the fall of 1905 that Ballin immediately ordered its kitchen doubled in size. But the marvel of a first-class à la carte restaurant, decorated in the classic style of Louis XVI, where one could dine superbly and intimately, was only half the story. On the *Amerika*, Mewès "was given the opportunity to achieve some kind of total design harmony," according to liner historian John Maxtone-Graham, "implementing a scheme of uniform decoration in all the public rooms throughout the ship." Aft of the restaurant, one entered an elegant lounge in the eighteenth-century style of Robert Adam. The airy Palm Court, with its blooming flowers, potted palms and white rattan furniture, was also inspired by Louis XVI. Only the dining room disappointed—its long tables, bolted swivel chairs and portholes draped with sateen were a throwback to an earlier era.

Amerika, which immediately became the most fashionable ship on the North Atlantic, set the stage for the heyday of liner grand luxe. Mewès went on to design the interiors of the *Amerika*'s sister ship, *Kaiserin Auguste Viktoria*, and then the three HAPAG giants of the *Imperator* class that outsized even White Star's famous, doomed *Titanic*. In this competitive climate, both White Star and Cunard realized that to maintain their share of the Atlantic passenger trade, they would have to build new ships of unprecedented size and luxury. The age of the Atlantic superliner had truly begun.

Luxe Germanica

By the turn of the nineteenth century, the two great German lines, Norddeutscher Lloyd and Hamburg-Amerika, had surpassed the British in both speed and luxury, but it was ornamentation rather than speed that came to predominate. At first, interior decoration tended toward the grandiose and the neo baroque, as can be seen from the Deutschland's grill room (top right) and the Kaiser Wilhelm II's grotesquely overwrought first class dining saloon (opposite). But, with the arrival of the more restrained aesthetic of French architect/designer Charles Mewès, German ship interiors acquired a sophistication and a unity of style hitherto unknown. The Winter Garden aboard the Kaiserin Auguste Viktoria (bottom right) shows Mewès at his delicate best. But even the master could fall prey to pomposity, witness his disappointing dining saloon on Amerika (middle right).

With the commissioning of both the *Lusitania* and the *Mauretania* in 1907, Cunard could boast the largest, fastest and most beautiful ships on the high seas.

The *Mauretania* went on to live a long and legendary life, but the *Lusitania* was cut down in her prime by a German torpedo, a catastrophe that may have hastened America's entry into World War I.

The Lusitania entering New York harbor at the end of an early crossing.

Friendly Rivals

The Story of the Lusitania *and the* Mauretania,
1907 ~ 1935

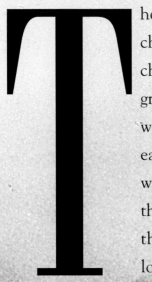

The rapid emergence of German liners as the North Atlantic champions for both speed and luxury left Great Britain's merchant marine in something of a state of shock. How could the greatest seafaring nation on earth, ruler of an empire on which the sun never had a chance to set, have been so easily and so emphatically eclipsed? To make matters worse, barely had the nineteenth century turned into the twentieth than America threatened to take over the North Atlantic passenger trade. For a time it looked as though all the great British

Above: *The* Lusitania *and the* Mauretania *heralded a new era of British dominance of what was known as the Atlantic Ferry. Their regular sailings from their home port of Liverpool came to epitomize Cunard's reputation for speed and reliability.*
Below: *The* Mauretania *(left) and the* Lusitania *pass each other in the Mersey off Liverpool.*

steamship lines—Cunard included—would fall under the sway of the legendary Yankee financier Junius Pierpont Morgan.

In 1901, J. P. Morgan formed International Mercantile Marine, whose holdings included Cunard's only serious British rival for the North Atlantic trade, the White Star Line. The major non-British lines, such as Holland-Amerika, were quick to make their peace with the emerging maritime colossus, among them HAPAG's canny Albert Ballin. When Ballin caught wind of Morgan's plans, he negotiated a deal guaranteeing his company's independence while granting the International Mercantile Marine a substantial interest in it. As part of this commercial treaty—kept secret until after it was a fait accompli—the two interests agreed to keep clear of each other's routes and to inaugurate new ones only after mutual consultation.

Such international business collusion, common in an era of unfettered capitalism, placed Cunard in what appeared to be an untenable situation. Unable to afford new ships ambitious enough to compete with the new Morgan shipping combine, Cunard appeared likely to be devoured too, gaining the American a virtual North Atlantic monopoly. Lord Inverclyde, Cunard's chairman, saw clearly that his only escape route was political. Skillfully playing to patriotic pride in Cunard's distinguished history and to the very real threat that Britain would soon be left without ownership of a single major shipping line, in 1902 he corralled the government into lending his company a low-interest twenty-year loan of £2,600,000 for the building of two big new ships that would not only regain the Blue Riband for Britain but restore Cunard to a primary place in the North Atlantic. In return for this loan and for an annual operating subsidy of £150,000, Cunard agreed that the company would remain in British hands and that the two ships would be designed with a double purpose. Their decks would sport reinforced emplacements for future guns, their coal bunkers would run along the sides of the hull, to help protect their boilers from shell fire, and their innards would house deep storage spaces that could be readily converted into magazines, making them easily transformed into armed merchant cruisers in the event of war—or so it was then believed. (It was still standard naval doctrine that merchant ships could make effective warships.)

The original tenders called for two ships 750 feet long by 78 feet at their widest point, with a designed speed of 24.5 knots—anything less in terms of speed would result in a reduction in the annual operating subsidy. Although the dimensions would change and the ships become longer and wider, they retained the conceptual sleekness that helped earn them the sobriquet ocean greyhounds. The Scottish firm of John Brown and Co., of Clydebank, won the contract for the future *Lusitania*. The Tyneside firm of Swan, Hunter, and Wigham Richardson would simultaneously build the *Mauretania*.

What follows is a story of a friendly rivalry between a Scottish builder and an English builder that continued between a Scottish-built ship and an English-built ship once they entered passenger-carrying service. Actual construction didn't commence until 1904, the first two years being given over to developing and refining designs that had been on various drawing boards since 1901, gradually growing in size and ambition.

Both firms had to work within the same essential specifications and meet the exacting contract requirements for speed and performance. One can imagine the

Above: *Though nearly identical in size and basic design, the two ships were quite different in appearance. Compare the Lusitania's hinge-topped ventilators (top) with the Mauretania's more conventional cowl vents (above).*
Below: *The Lusitania's three-bladed props, which had blades bolted in place, never performed as well as the Mauretania's four-bladed versions.*

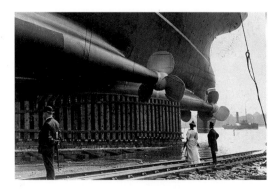

The Lusitania's launch at Clydebank on June 7, 1906, attracted 20,000 spectators, 600 of whom enjoyed a lavish post-launch luncheon in the shipyard's specially decorated molding loft, the vast building where the ship's skeleton was literally roughed out in chalk. Only the absence of Cunard's recently deceased chairman, Lord Inverclyde, sounded a melancholy note on an otherwise joyous occasion.

designers and engineers at each company poring over plans and debating the design niceties that would make their ship superior—and above all, faster—than its sister. In deciding the optimum contour for the hull, both firms had access to test data from the Admiralty tanks at Haslar. Dissatisfied with these tests, Swan Hunter built a wooden scale model, driven by electric motors, that ran incessantly up and down a quarter-mile stretch of the Tyne each time a slight variation in hull form needed to be tested.

The two ships that began to grow in their respective shipyards in the fall of 1904 were to an untutored eye identical. But there were differences. *Mauretania*'s rounded after end added some 5 feet to her overall length (790 feet to the *Lusitania*'s 785, and she came in at 31,938 gross tons to *Lusitania*'s 31,550), narrowly giving her boasting rights as the longer and larger ship. (Gross tons is a measure of the ship's cubic capacity, not weight.) No evidence suggests that this difference was a deliberate attempt by the English builders to have the bigger ship—*Mauretania* also drew an additional 1.5 inches—but the speculation is irresistible.

Of far more substance, as events would prove, was the difference in the design of the propellers. The *Lusitania*'s three-bladed propellers never performed as well as their designers hoped and were no match for the more efficient four-bladed props on the *Mauretania*. Possibly significant—though this has never been proved—were differences in the engine machinery and boilers. Cunard seems to have permitted some leeway in order to encourage the rival shipyards to experiment for best results.

Other differences did not affect performance, but they definitely contributed to the ships' distinct characters. For example, the *Lusitania*'s canisterlike hinge-topped ventilators gave her decks a cleaner and less cluttered look than the *Mauretania*'s traditional cowl ventilators. (Unfortunately the *Lusitania*'s vents weren't up to the rigors of the North Atlantic and needed constant replacing.) The porthole arrangements were different. The windows on the *Lusitania* were slightly rounded at the top and the bottom; the *Mauretania*'s formed simple rectangles. Most noticeable to the passengers who came to know both ships, however, were the differences in their interior designs.

Unlike the rival White Star Line, Cunard had a long tradition of creating a different look for the passenger areas of each new ship. Although starting from identical deck plans for the public rooms and cabins, the two designers—James Millar on the

Nothing demonstrates the contrasting interior design scheme of the two ships better than their splendid, domed dining saloons.
Above and bottom: *The Mauretania's first-class saloon.*
Below and right: *The same room on the Lusitania.*

Lusitania and Harold Peto on the *Mauretania*—created ships with quite distinct atmospheres. Millar, a Scottish architect perhaps influenced by the work of Charles Mewès on HAPAG's recent *Amerika*, produced a ship with a lighter, more delicate, more refined feel. Based on the simple lines of the Georgian period and Louis XVI style, the design featured white plaster highlighted by gold leaf. One writer refers to the *Lusitania*'s style as one of "cool elegance." By contrast, Peto, a noted designer of contemporary English manor houses, took his cue from the English baronial tradition of shipboard interior design. Lavish in their use of oak and mahogany, Peto's interiors gave the *Mauretania* a darker, heavier feel. The hand-carved paneling on the *Mauretania* became famous; in the dining saloon, done up in the style of François I, each panel was unique.

These were the most luxurious Cunarders built so far—the *Lusitania*'s second-class public rooms closely resembled Cunard's first-class rooms of a few years earlier—but comfort in the modern sense was still a good way off. For all their differences, both ships continued the English tradition of stylistic eclecticism, mixing historical periods at random. In their showpiece dining rooms, swivel chairs remained bolted to the floor. There was no room on these sleek vessels built above all for speed for the increase in privacy provided by more intimate dining alcoves. If you were unlucky enough to land a seat too close or too far from the table, there was nothing you could do. And private bathrooms were still a rarity reserved for only the classiest of first-class staterooms. Nonetheless, when the *Lusitania* and *Mauretania* entered service, they could claim to be the most luxurious passenger ships in the world.

But it was speed that would earn them their fame, and the quest for speed explained the decision to install what was still an experimental technology in the engine rooms of both ships. For the first time the largest passenger liners in the world would be powered by steam turbines.

A scant ten years earlier, no shipping magnate worth his balance sheet would have wagered a halfpenny on such a stunning turn of events, not until the Royal Naval Review at Spithead in June 1897, the year of Queen Victoria's Diamond Jubilee. At that event, with the Prince of Wales looking on, a tiny turbine-powered craft named

Top: *The Mauretania's first-class lounge and music room displayed the lavish use of wood typical of the ship's interiors.* Above: *The Lusitania's lounge relied on plaster work and natural light to give it a more spacious and airy feel.*

Turbinia had darted indecorously among the assembled battleships of the British Home Fleet, embarrassing the naval bigwigs but garnering headlines and credibility by its brash feat. The little ship, belching fire and smoke from its single stack and outracing the swiftest of the Royal Navy's torpedo boats, was the brainchild of a gentleman engineer named Charles Parsons, and the steam turbines that powered it were his innovation. (The turbine was not a new idea; using it to propel a ship was.) Soon the Royal Navy had two turbine-powered ships; then smaller passenger liners successfully adopted the new technology. But it was a giant step to put engines so relatively untested into ships meant to recapture Cunard's and Britain's mercantile prestige.

Above: *The* Turbinia, *the world's first turbine-powered ship.*
Right: *The* Lusitania *steaming eastbound off the Irish coast.*

Nonetheless as the two ships on the drawing boards grew in size, and ever-faster German ships maintained their grasp on the Blue Riband, it seemed that turbine power might provide the decisive competitive edge. But would the new technology deliver the 68,000 horsepower required for the *Lusitania* and the *Mauretania*? Would it deliver the power but at too high a price in coal consumed? Would the massive turbines perform reliably with minimal maintenance on ships so large? (Cunard tested turbines on the *Carmania*, launched in 1905, which consistently outperformed her identical sister *Caronia*, equipped with traditional reciprocating engines.) Yet in the end, the committee charged with deciding this vexing question gave the go-ahead. Either these ships would exceed even their builders' expectations or they would end up not as ocean greyhounds but as huge and costly white elephants.

First down the slips was the *Lusitania*, launched by Lady Inverclyde to cheering thousands in June of 1906, fitted out and ready for a series of secret builders' trials by the mid-summer of 1907. Although no official record of these tests survives, the results were far from satisfactory in one respect. At high speeds, the *Lusitania*'s stern vibrated so badly that many second-class passengers were going to find their quarters uninhabitable. The vibrations were mainly a result of the turbulence caused by the four huge

propellers. The science of propeller design was still in its developmental stages.

Lusitania returned to Clydebank for some fairly major interior renovations. Airy second-class public rooms were transformed into a severely subdivided warren of beams, pillars and arches designed to stiffen the stern and reduce the shaking. These helped, but vibration would remain a problem throughout her career.

Speed, on the other hand was never a problem for either of these nearly identical sisters. On *Lusitania*'s official trials in July 1907, she regularly exceeded 26 knots for extended distances, well above her designed speed of 24.5 knots. This boded well for a record Atlantic crossing. But her maiden voyage in September proved a bit of disappointment. Sporadic fog, including a heavy fog bank on the final day, slowed her down, and she arrived off Sandy Hook, then the entrance to New York harbor, thirty minutes shy of the existing record, still held by the Germans. When she entered New York harbor, she did so by means of a new channel expressly dredged to accommodate her unprecedented size. Dock renovations and dredging had also been required at her Liverpool home base. In the years to come, harbors and port facilities on both sides of the Atlantic would repeatedly require costly upgrades as the superliners grew ever larger.

While *Lusitania* was making her maiden crossing, the *Mauretania* was nearing readiness. Her secret trials had likewise revealed a problem with vibration, in her case worst in the forward superstructure. Humfrey Jordan, in his delightful chronicle of the *Mauretania*'s long and brilliant career, describes the puzzlement in the engine room when the ship's commander suddenly and inexplicably ordered the engines slowed during a high-speed run. When queried on this decision, the captain is said to have replied, "Because I was being shaken off my bridge." And so the second ship had returned to her fitting-out basin for some necessary adjustment. But the vibration problem was never as severe in the *Mauretania*, and the renovations she needed not as radical as those the *Lusitania* underwent.

In the official trials before she was accepted and commissioned by Cunard, the *Mauretania* performed slightly better than had her sister, averaging a little more than 26 knots over a distance exceeding a thousand miles. Already the

"LUSITANIA" PASSING OLD HEAD OF KINSALE

CUNARD LINE

Above: *The Lusitania's maiden crossing from Liverpool to New York disappointed those anticipating a new westbound speed record, but was otherwise a resounding success. An estimated 200,000 well-wishers saw her off from Merseyside, and her shipboard amenities garnered encomiums such as the following from the* Marine Engineer: *"Of the hundreds of passengers who made a successful trip on her memorable maiden voyage, how many could say that they had ever had so luxurious a time in their lives?"*

Mauretania seemed marked as the favored ship.

By the time the *Mauretania* began her maiden voyage on November 16, 1907, the *Lusitania* had finally snatched the Blue Riband from the Germans, making the passage from Queenstown, Ireland, to New York in four days, nineteen hours and fifty-two minutes at an average speed fractionally under 24 knots. It was the first time a ship had crossed the Atlantic in under five days.

The big crowd that witnessed the *Mauretania's* maiden departure from Liverpool on that rainy, mist-shrouded November day fully expected a new record. But November is not an ideal month for Atlantic speeding, particularly not in the teeth of an old-fashioned North Atlantic westerly gale. As the brand-new ship fought her way westward, huge seas broke over her bow and her passengers retreated to their cabins.

Any who imagined that these vast new vessels would somehow transcend a storm at sea discovered, if anything, the opposite. The *Mauretania*, whose slender beam and dagger bow were meant for speed and speed above all, pitched and rolled dramatically—but she managed to maintain good speed until a wave dislodged a spare anchor on the foredeck. This mishap forced the ship to heave to amid mountainous seas while the errant anchor was lashed down, dashing any hopes of a record maiden run. But after the gale passed and the seas subsided, she managed the first of her many feats of fleetness, covering 624 miles in a single day, 6 more than the *Lusitania*'s best daily run and thus the fastest single day's voyage in history.

Nor was it long before the *Mauretania* snatched a piece of the Blue Riband for herself. On her homebound voyage she shaved twenty-four minutes off the *Lusitania*'s eastbound record. The event marked the start of an unofficial but very real race between the two Cunarders, one that fascinated the general public although its existence was piously disclaimed by the Cunard Company. Soon it seemed that each time the *Lusitania* broke her sister's record, the *Mauretania* would come back with a slightly faster time. Other great ships appeared to lure passengers away, but none attempted to compete for speed, so decisively had the two Cunarders raised the ante. No one could have guessed it at the time, but the Blue Riband first won by these two ships in 1907 would remain their property for the next twenty-two years.

By the time the Mauretania *departed Tyneside for her secret trials in late October of 1907, her sister* Lusitania *had finally snatched the Blue Riband from the Germans. But the* Mauretania *would not be long in overtaking her.*

More important, though less glamorous, became their reputation for reliability, a hallmark of the Cunard Company ever since Samuel Cunard's first four steamers went into service in the early 1840s. Regardless of weather, the two new Cunarders got through. They may have occasionally arrived late after battling an Atlantic gale, but they always left at or close to the appointed time, regularly making their round trips between Liverpool and New York in sixteen or seventeen days, including a five-day turnaround in New York. A major recoaling was required before the return passage, but to the company's surprise and pleasure, the new turbines used less than the predicted thousand tons of coal a day.

This reputation for reliability and punctuality was put to a stern test in December

Many observers concluded that the Aquitania (below) marked the peak of maritime interior design before the war, with her pleasing (to the late-Edwardian eye) eclecticism. The cutaway (bottom) is intended to impress us with her extraordinary facilities and astounding decorative flourishes. Reportedly the ship's crowning glory was her Palladian lounge, done up in a style reminiscent of the work of the great English architect Christopher Wren.

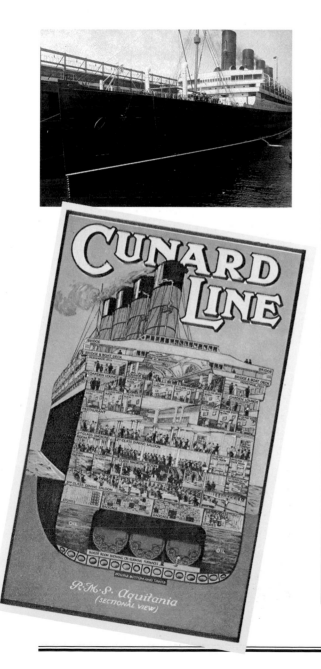

1910, when Cunard announced that the *Mauretania* would make a special pre-Christmas voyage, an unprecedented round-trip passage in twelve days. The usual five-days turnaround would be compressed to only forty-eight hours. Her German rivals scoffed. The stormy North Atlantic did its best to wreck her plans, but even though she arrived late and had to make her turnaround, including the laborious process of coaling, in an unheard-of thirty hours, she left on schedule and delivered her passengers to Britain in time for Christmas. Not to be outdone, in 1911, the *Lusitania* made a record sixteen round-trip voyages. More remarkable still, from 1909 to 1911 the *Mauretania* was in continuous service without a major reconditioning.

Because the *Lusitania*'s career would be cut short by a German torpedo, we have no way of knowing whether their rivalry for reliability would have survived into the postwar years. Certainly the *Mauretania* proved a paragon in this respect. Her most famous captain, Arthur Rostron, the man who in April 1912 raced the *Carpathia* to rescue the *Titanic* survivors, reports in his memoirs that the Tuesday 3:15 train from Southampton to Liverpool was jokingly called the Rostron Express. (By the twenties, following White Star's lead, Cunard had switched its main terminus from Liverpool to Southampton.) If Rostron's ship arrived on schedule, he could easily make this train and be home in Liverpool for dinner. In his nine years as the *Mauretania*'s peacetime skipper, he claims he missed his usual train only once.

Reliable, yes, fast, indubitably, but as the *Mauretania*'s maiden voyage revealed, both new Cunarders could be quite uncomfortable ships, especially in heavy seas. They were "wet ships," so constructed that their bows plunged into an oncoming wave rather than riding above it and often sending great lashings of spray as high as the bridge. (During a crossing in January 1910, the *Lusitania* encountered a giant rogue wave so powerful that it slammed the bridge aft by several inches.) Again it was the shape of the bow that was to blame, the way it rose straight up rather than flaring out as it rose. But the particular pitch and roll of these two greyhounds contributed to their distinctive characters. Humfrey Jordan relates that even in a relatively calm sea the *Mauretania* had a mischievous habit of pitching and spraying without warning, on more than one occasion dousing the commander when he was making a brief stop on the bridge before descending to dinner in his blue-and-gold dress uniform. To the men who captained her, it was as if the ship were playing a deliberate practical joke.

Although vibration inevitably came with speed, *Mauretania*'s vibration problem was further reduced in early 1909 when she was fitted with a set of new propellers. (She had lost one during a westward crossing in May 1908 and had finished out the season with only three.) The blades of the original props had been bolted in place; the new propellers came from a single cast. The change not only decreased vibration but made her markedly faster—enough to convince Cunard that the *Lusitania*'s three-bladed props also warranted replacement. But even with both ships bearing identical screws, *Mauretania*'s dominance continued—though not in the passenger popularity department. Before the war, *Lusitania* was the more popular ship, a fact easily forgotten because of her sister's longer life. Presumably this has something to do with her more airy interior decor.

As dominant as these two ships were in the years before World War I, they lacked one essential ingredient: a worthy operating partner. Given the seventeen days—including turnaround time—required to make a complete round-trip voyage, plus a good week in Liverpool to prepare for the next voyage, only a third great ship could enable Cunard to guarantee weekly sailings from either side of the Atlantic. Cunard's answer was the 45,647 ton *Aquitania*.

When the *Aquitania* entered service in June of 1914, only two months before the outbreak of war, she represented both a departure for Cunard and a contrast to *Lusitania* and *Mauretania*. Although she was able to make 24 knots, she would never wear a Blue Riband. She was bigger and broader, built for comfort and decorated to the hilt, meant to out-luxe the increasing luxurious competition that was drawing passengers away from Cunard. From her first-class suites inspired by famous painters (Rembrandt, Holbein, Van Dyck, Velasquez and others) to her grandiose public rooms that seemed to cover every imaginable decorative style from every important historical period going as far back as ancient Rome, she resembled, in the words of John Malcolm Brinnin, "a sea-going museum."

The outbreak of World War I nipped Cunard's nascent three-ship service in the bud and cut short the friendly peacetime rivalry of the *Mauretania* and the *Lusitania*. Those who expected the sisters to continue their competition as armed merchant

The Aquitania may have been somewhat slower than Cunard's two ocean greyhounds, but she was even more luxurious and, with her slightly broader beam, more stable in rough weather.

cruisers soon had their expectations dashed. In August 1914, the German liner *Kaiser Wilhelm der Grosse*, which had been converted to an auxiliary cruiser, was attacked while refueling at sea by the British *Campania*, herself a converted Cunard liner. *Campania* sank the *Kaiser*, but was so badly damaged in the exchange that repairs took about a year. This early demonstration of the vulnerability of converted express liners, combined with the huge amounts of expensive fuel they required, which also limited their range, sealed their fate as warships. The British Admiralty, which had laid down such strict requirements during their construction, almost immediately abandoned the notion of auxiliary cruisers in the face of wartime reality.

Instead the opening months of the conflict found the *Mauretania* stripped of her rich appointments, her fancy furniture lodged in a warehouse while she sat idly waiting for the Admiralty to decide what to do with her. Meanwhile, the *Lusitania* continued traveling the traditional North Atlantic run between Liverpool and New York, completing one round trip a month. Although a noncombatant, she was a British ship, making her a potential target for German U-boats. But in those early days of the war, few believed the Germans would sink an unarmed passenger vessel. And even though six boilers had been shut down to conserve fuel, she was still the fastest ship traveling between England and America, having a maximum of speed of 21 knots.

The *Lusitania* carried a healthy complement of American passengers when she departed New York for Liverpool on May 1, 1915, despite a published warning from the German authorities that appeared in U.S. newspapers the morning of her departure. By this time a number of British merchant ships had been sunk by German subs, but the famous liner's speed still seemed the best guarantee of safety. Certainly her captain and crew should have been on high alert. As the *Lusitania* neared the end of her crossing, a German U-boat sank three British ships in the waters south of Ireland through which she was about to sail, and he received repeated warnings that U-boats were active on his intended course. Yet on May 7, as the *Lusitania* entered the most dangerous part of her passage, Captain William Turner actually slowed down, apparently worried by patchy fog.

In fact, Turner was ignoring or at least bending every one of the Admiralty's directives for evading German submarines. He was steaming too close to shore, where

© **KEN MARSCHALL**

Right: *Few of the almost two thousand passengers who left New York aboard the* Lusitania *on May 1, 1915, seemed concerned about the grim warning from Germany that had appeared in U.S. newspapers the morning of her departure.* Far right: *Popular legend says this photograph shows American nurses aboard the* Lusitania *on her final voyage.*

U-boats loved to lurk, instead of in the relative safety of the open channel. He was sailing at less than top speed, and he wasn't zigzagging (later he claimed to believe that zigzagging was a tactic to be adopted only *after* a U-boat was sighted). In his defense, it must be stated that Turner was steering the *Lusitania* farther from shore than had the ship's previous commander on several wartime crossings. And his many years as a merchant captain undoubtedly inclined him to trust his own instincts over bureaucratic directives he didn't fully understand. It can also be argued that so important a ship merited a destroyer escort for the most perilous part of its voyage.

Whether or not Turner's behavior can be justified, it doomed his ship. When *U-20* under the command of Kapitänleutnant Walther Schwieger found a huge four-stacker in its sights just south of Queenstown, Ireland, it was able to kill her with a single torpedo, penetrating the hull just below the waterline. The initial explosion set off a violent secondary blast. The ship sank in eighteen minutes, with a loss of 1,195 of the 1,959 on board, including 123 Americans. Captain Turner was washed clear of the bridge as the ship sank, and survived after spending more than three hours in the water.

Above: *Some have faulted Captain William Turner's conduct during the Lusitania's final voyage.* **Left:** *The fatal torpedo finds its target.*

The loss of the *Lusitania* provoked great outrage in the United States and helped create the climate of public opinion that would later allow America to join the war. It also marked the end of any delusions that the "civilized" manners of nineteenth-century warfare could survive into the twentieth.

When the *Lusitania* went down, the *Mauretania* was carrying her first load of British troops for the ill-starred landings at Gallipoli. Before war's end, she would transport more than fifty thousand soldiers, most of them Americans. She also served briefly as a hospital ship during the Gallipoli campaign. And although she had some close shaves, she was never damaged and never lost a life because of enemy fire or navigational

error. In part this can be attributed to luck, but part of this luck must stem from the quality of her commanders. On one of her Mediterranean voyages she missed a torpedo by roughly five feet. Only the quick reaction of Captain David Dow when he spotted the telltale wake and ordered the helm hard to port saved the *Mauretania* from sharing her sister's fate. And *Mauretania*'s best days were yet to come.

This rosy future was not evident, however, when she reentered regular passenger service in March 1920, now operating from Southampton. Her posh furniture and hand-carved paneling had been restored to their rightful places, but she was not the ocean racer of yore, now often unable to match speeds with her more commodious competition. On her second voyage to New York in 1920 she averaged a miserable 17.81 knots, a showing that could not be blamed entirely on the postwar shortage of good coal and the scarcity of

Left: *The Lusitania's final moments. Her sister* Mauretania (above) *served as both a hospital ship and trooper.*

men willing and able to endure the hard labor of the stokehold. On no single passage in that first postwar year did she average more than 22 knots. The *Mauretania* suddenly seemed behind the times and in danger of falling out of fashion. She badly needed a major overhaul, but the company needed the profits from her reliable performance.

Just when she seemed likely to fade into mediocrity, fate intervened. In July 1921 a fire caused by inflammable cleaning fluid did enough damage to the first-class accommodations to force cancellation of her next voyage at the height of her busiest season. Cunard took this opportunity to make the expensive and farsighted conversion from coal to oil. When she returned to service, she was a faster ship, but still not her prewar self.

In late 1923, Cunard took the second necessary step to restore the *Mauretania* to glory. They ordered her into port for a complete overhaul of her once-revolutionary but now sadly worn-out turbines. The work went well and was almost complete when the

English workers on the job went out on strike. So it fell to Captain Arthur Rostron to command his ship on the strangest voyage she ever attempted to make—from Southampton to Cherbourg under tugboat power. In Cherbourg, French workmen would finish the job.

The trip went smoothly until the French coast was in view. Then the wind shifted to the west and blew up a moderate gale. Rostron's first concern was keeping the unloaded ship upright, since any serious list would wreak havoc with the disassembled turbines. But the wind was more than the six Dutch tugs could handle. Rostron remembered it well: "By two o'clock we were going astern with a five-knot tide against us. Nothing could be done and we were only two miles off the rocks near Cape Barfleur!" The captain felt "fairly confident" the tide would turn in time. It did. And so did the *Mauretania*'s fortunes.

Near the end of her days, the Mauretania was painted white for cruising in tropical climes. She was finally withdrawn from service in the fall of 1934 and spent the long winter of 1934–35 resting quietly at dockside in Southampton. That spring she was sold for scrap and her fittings were auctioned off. Her famous paneling went to the backers of a planned Hotel Mauretania in New York City, a project that never materialized. Some found its way into a pub in Bristol, England.

The Mauretania *enters port for the last time as she arrives at Rosyth at the end of her voyage to the wreckers, an occasion that inspired much purple journalese, including the following: "The final link with the world she has roved so long is broken and the* Mauretania *is sailing away to the port from which there is no return. From across the darkening Southampton water the deep, sudden voices of big ships lament her. . . It is a final, irrevocable good-bye."*

For the rest of the 1920s, until 1926 under Rostron's able command, she was once again the class of the Atlantic run. Other ships might have been smoother and more comfy, but none could beat her. In August 1924 Rostron guided her from New York to Cherbourg at an average speed of 26.19 knots, breaking her prewar record and cementing her postwar reputation. She would remain the unchallenged speed queen of the seas until 1929.

But all great careers must come to an end. When, inevitably, the *Mauretania* lost the Blue Riband to a younger, more technologically advanced ship, her days as a great transatlantic liner were numbered. Despite a major renovation in the winter of 1926-27 that refitted one hundred staterooms, adding many private baths, and redecorated and refurbished her public spaces, she could not catch up with her competition in terms of the comfort and amenities now considered de rigueur, such as a swimming pool. With transatlantic passenger service down because of the Depression, she increasingly saw service as a cruising ship, taking Britons to the Mediterranean and Americans to the Caribbean. Among her least glorious missions were Prohibition-era "booze cruises" from New York to Nassau and back.

Cunard withdrew the *Mauretania* from service in September 1934. For almost a year she lay rusting in Southampton harbor while her owners debated her fate. Finally, her fittings were auctioned off, and on July 1, 1935, she began her final voyage to Rosyth, Scotland, where her hull would be sold for scrap. But no one could purchase her soul.

Her former commander, now Sir Arthur Rostron, K.B.E., late commodore of the Cunard Line, saw her off from the quay, but he would not go on board. "I prefer to remember her as she was in her best days," he said simply. Like so many captains before and since, he had fallen in love with an inanimate assemblage of metal and wood. She had assumed a personality and a life of her own. In his memoirs Rostron spends many pages describing his years on *Mauretania* and devotes only a sentence or two to his final command, the magnificent *Berengaria*, "the most comfortable ship I was ever in." The *Mauretania*, like her long-departed sister the *Lusitania*, could be a difficult ship, an unpredictable ship, an uncomfortable ship, but to Rostron she was from the first and to the last "a lady."

Exploring the *Lusitania*

We came to the wreck of the *Lusitania* in the summer of 1993 hoping to solve its greatest mystery: what caused the violent secondary explosion that undoubtedly led the ship to sink so quickly? Some have argued that it was contraband munitions. Conspiracy theorists have even claimed that the British sank the ship deliberately to hasten America's entry into the war. But even if we found no "smoking gun" on the seafloor off the southern Irish coast, our technology would allow us to bring back a

complete visual record of what remains of this great lost liner, preserving her for posterity.

Unfortunately for our investigation, previous visitors had already tampered with the evidence. The wreck lies in just 295 feet of water, making it relatively easy pickings. Reports of blasting and salvaging operations, some apparently conducted by or for the Royal Navy, dated back to 1946. In the 1980s salvagers had removed two of the bow anchors and three of the four bronze propellers. But nothing prepared us for the actual scene of devastation.

The hull is in two torn and twisted pieces, a sad echo of its former glory. It is probable that the bow section tore free of the rest of the ship when it hit bottom. The wreck is pocked with holes that were probably caused by depth charges. The *Lusitania* lies on her starboard side, obscuring the area where the torpedo hit, but our careful *(Continued on page 66)*

Opposite: *The tiny* Delta *submarine explores the sunken* Lusitania*'s bow, now a distorted remnant of the original.*
Top: Delta *zeroes in on the bow.*
Above:*The letter* A *from the* Lusitania*'s name.*

1　2　3

4

The wreck of the Lusitania *looks like a battlefield the day after, yet many of her original features are still recognizable.*

1) A hinge-topped vent with visible remains of the mechanism for opening and closing the lid.

2) A piece of the ship's rail, now detached from the hull.

3) The telemotor control from the ship's bridge.

4) A bathtub, with shower fixture still attached, stands beside a skylight.

5) The ship's telegraph from the aft docking bridge.

5

inspection of the port side of the hull revealed no evidence of the gaping hole reported by scuba diver John Light who made numerous dives to the wreck in the early 1960s. We also discovered that the hull has collapsed to roughly half its original width.

This fact helps explain how the superstructure has become such a chaotic disaster area, where almost nothing is

recognizable. The decks have slid down to starboard and much of the upperworks of the ship has collapsed into a heap of rubble on the seafloor. To make matters worse, the forecastle was festooned with fishing nets, making this part of the upperworks extremely dangerous for our vehicles to explore. Only the foremost part of the bow seemed somewhat recognizable as belonging to the famous Blue Riband holder. The bow is upturned, to an angle of about 45 degrees, and the outline of the ship's name is visible—one of the biggest highlights of our exploration.

Directing exploration operations on the *Lusitania* wreck was a little like parading a marching band through a minefield at midnight—literally as well as metaphorically, since we saw a number of unexploded depth charges, presumably a remnant of Irish naval exercises. I constantly had to worry where each of our three vehicles was. And because the wreck lies close to shore, there are strong tidal currents that can play havoc with underwater positioning and cloud the area with sediment. Despite all our care, we had at least one underwater

collision and several near misses. And those nets were hellish. At one point our tiny submarine *Delta*, with three people onboard, sucked a net into its propeller and had to drop its tail to escape. On another occasion, divers had to cut *Jason* free of nets in which it had become caught.

In the end we sailed home with many haunting images of the wreck, including a single ladies' shoe and a bathtub complete with shower apparatus. But we found nothing to suggest the ship was sabotaged. Nor was there any evidence of an explosion in the area of the ship's magazine, which is presumably where contraband munitions, if any, would have been stowed. The other strong possibility, a boiler explosion, seems highly unlikely since none was reported by any of the survivors from the three boiler rooms in operation. We finally concluded that the only real clues to the cause of the secondary explosion were the many lumps of coal that lay scattered across the seafloor near the ship and must have fallen from her as she sank.

The torpedo likely ripped open the ship at one of the starboard coal bunkers, nearly empty at the end of the transatlantic crossing. The violent impact kicked up clouds of coal dust, which when mixed with oxygen and touched by fire becomes an explosive combination. The resulting blast, the reported second explosion, ripped open the starboard side of the hull and doomed the ship.

So ended the life of the *Lusitania*. She is now a faint ghost of the ocean greyhound she once was, one of the saddest wrecks I've ever seen. But when I visualize her upturned bow, I can imagine the pride of those who once sailed on the swiftest ship in the world.

Inset far left: *I stand beside one of the Lusitania's salvaged propellers.*
Left: *A stateroom window with filigree.*
Right: *Floor tile.*
Far right: *The remains of a ladies' shoe.*
Below: Delta *and our two robot vehicles explore the hull rupture that opens into what were once the ship's boiler rooms.*

Chapter 3

With the *Olympic* and the *Titanic*, the White Star Line looked to have trumped the opposition. But the *Titanic*'s fatal appointment with an iceberg on that now-famous April night not only seriously damaged White Star's reputation, it shook the confidence of an era infatuated by wealth and technological progress.

The Titanic *speeds seaward on her maiden voyage.*

Death of a Dream

The Saga of the Olympic *and the* Titanic, 1911 ~ 1935

White Star Line R. M. S. Titanic

White Star Line R. M. S. Olympic

Even in our age of radar and satellite positioning, fog is still a treacherous enemy for any mariner. In the early years of the century, when shipping lanes were growing increasingly crowded with ever faster and bigger vessels, fog was the North Atlantic sea captain's worst nightmare, even greater than his fear of ice. Before the invention of wireless, a ship could simply disappear without an epitaph—and thousands did. No one knows how many of these lost ships—"never heard from," in the seaman's vernacular—collided with another vessel or with an invisible ice mountain and sank in fog. Days would drag into weeks before all hope was abandoned and the ship was given up as gone for good.

By the time Cunard's *Lusitania* and *Mauretania* began to ply the North Atlantic, however, these traditional hazards had begun to seem less dire. The new superliners were built of steel, had double bottoms to reduce the chances of water penetrating the ship's innards and were subdivided into watertight compartments. In theory, even if several of these sections were breached, the ship would remain afloat. If it sank, it would go down so slowly that a wireless distress call would bring help in ample time. It is hardly surprising, therefore, given the intense competition between lines and liners

The White Star Line's Republic *could not compete with the* Mauretania *or* Lusitania *in terms of speed or luxury, but she was considered a safe and solid ship until she was rammed in 1909. Unlike most White Star ships, she had been purchased from another line, but in keeping with company tradition, her builder was the ever-reliable Harland & Wolff of Belfast.*

in the North Atlantic, that experienced captains began to take the calculated risk of steaming at high speeds through regions of fog or ice.

Such a commander was Captain William Sealby of the White Star Line's *Republic*, a 15,378-ton passenger steamer just out of New York en route to the Mediterranean carrying 742 passengers and crew. In the early morning of January 23, 1909, she was southwest of Nantucket Island, steaming blind through a wet blanket of fog. Sealby alerted his engine room but reduced his speed only marginally, blowing the ship's whistle at regular intervals to alert other vessels to his presence. As was customary, the captain did not leave the bridge; he would stay there until the fog had lifted.

At 5:47 a.m., Captain Sealby and the other officers on duty heard a ship's whistle just off the port bow—almost dead ahead. Sealby ordered the ship's engines full astern and the helm hard-a-port, signaling his maneuver with two blasts from the ship's whistle, but it was too late. A vessel emerged from the fog and rammed the *Republic* almost at right angles and roughly amidships, killing three passengers asleep in their bunks and leaving its anchor in one of the staterooms before breaking free. In a matter of minutes, the *Republic*'s engine rooms and boiler rooms were flooded and she had developed an alarming list. Power failed and all the lights went out. Meanwhile the *Republic*'s anonymous assailant drifted back into the fog.

Sealby seems to have remained remarkably calm under the circumstances and remarkably confident his ship would stay afloat. He mustered the remainder of his 442 passengers on the sloping deck, offering them hot coffee and blankets while he reassured them that rescue was on the way. Thanks to the presence of a new Marconi set on board and to the fine work of radioman Jack Binns, it was.

Binns had been asleep at the time of the collision and awoke to find his radio cabin in ruins around him and the ship's power gone. He immediately rigged up the emergency batteries and began to transmit the standard distress signal, CQD—the first time in history a ship in trouble had radioed a call for help. His call was picked up on Nantucket and relayed to several ships not far away, including White Star's *Baltic*, which immediately poured on steam and headed for the *Republic*'s position.

In the end, the *Republic*'s passengers were rescued twice. First on the scene was the

Below: *The Republic (center) attended by (left) the New York and (right) the Cunard liner Lucania, just two of the ships that answered her radioed distress call.* **Right:** *Captain Sealby and a handful of his crew remain on the poop deck, still hoping to save their ship after her passengers had been evacuated.*

Florida, the ship that had rammed them. Remarkably, the smaller Lloyd Italiano liner, carrying nine hundred Italian immigrants to America, many of them survivors of the devastating Messina earthquake, remained afloat. Her bow had been crumpled right back to a collision bulkhead, but that had held. Now the *Florida* groped her way back

to the *Republic* through the fog. After a laborious transfer in a choppy sea had taken place, only a skeleton crew remained on board the *Republic* and the *Florida* was dangerously overloaded. But the *Baltic*, which had arrived in the vicinity, was now lost in the fog herself and drifted for many hours before she found her way to the *Republic* around 7:00 p.m. Now both the *Republic*'s and the *Florida*'s passengers were taken aboard the larger, undamaged ship, which was fortunately traveling with many empty cabins.

This time the process did not go so smoothly, owing to a combination of British class consciousness and early-twentieth-century Anglo-Saxon racism. After the *Republic*'s women and children had been safely transferred, the first-class men took their turn—ahead of all "foreigners," whether male or female. In response, the frightened and outraged Italians nearly rioted. "Discipline, however, was maintained and the privilege of class upheld," one of the *Republic*'s officers later wrote.

When everyone was safely brought on board, the *Baltic* steamed for New York while Captain Sealby endeavored to save the still-floating *Republic*, on which the intrepid radio operator remained almost to the last, making him a huge, if temporary, celebrity when he reached New York. But an attempt to tow the wounded vessel into shallow water ultimately failed, and roughly thirty-six hours after she had been struck, she sank.

Although the *Republic* was then the largest ship ever to have found an Atlantic grave, her loss seems if anything to have increased the confidence of shipowners and their employees. Thanks to her twelve watertight compartments, she had sunk slowly. A wireless distress call had brought an entire flotilla of ships to her side—though only two had participated in the rescue—and all but three of her passengers had got off safely. (Three of *Florida*'s crewmen died in the collision.) But Captain Sealby had been lucky. His ship had been rammed by a smaller ship with a weakly constructed bow. And one of his engineers had acted heroically to slowly cool the boilers so as to prevent them from exploding. No one could guarantee the next ship would be so fortunate.

But this was the Edwardian era, when Progress seemed inexorable and Technology about to conquer all. A year and a half before the *Republic* sank, the White Star Line had embarked on its most ambitious shipbuilding enterprise ever, one that promised in the eyes of some to make the idea of a shipwreck forever obsolete.

In the summer of 1907, the English papers were full of the impending maiden voyage of the *Lusitania*, then undergoing her acceptance trials, and of her soon-to-be-completed sister, *Mauretania*. Cunard seemed poised to skim the cream off the lucrative transatlantic carriage trade, a prospect not pleasing to J. Bruce Ismay, the man who ran the White Star Line, Cunard's chief rival. Thus, on the summer evening when Ismay escorted his wife to dinner at the Belgravia mansion of Lord William James Pirrie, it was inevitable that talk would turn to White Star's next move. Lord Pirrie was the driving force behind the great success of the Belfast shipbuilders Harland & Wolff, responsible for the building of all of White Star's ships. Now that White Star was controlled by J. P. Morgan's International Mercantile Marine, these two allies could count on an almost unlimited supply of capital to back any scheme.

According to legend, over after-dinner brandy and cigars, the two men sketched their plans for two ships of unprecedented size, half again as large as the new Cunarders

Opposite: *J. Bruce Ismay (top), managing director of the White Star Line, and Lord William James Pirrie of Harland & Wolff conceived the idea for the* Olympic *and her sister the* Titanic. Above: *The world's two largest ships take shape side-by-side in their stocks at the Belfast shipyards of Harland & Wolff. As the* Olympic *nears completion, the hull of the* Titanic *has already assumed its final shape.*

and bigger than any British shipyard facility then in existence could build. No attempt would be made to compete with the *Lusitania* and *Mauretania* in terms of speed. The new ships' selling points would be the comfort and luxury that came with their great size. But thanks to their twin reciprocating engines, the largest in the world, and a smaller low-pressure turbine, they would be fast enough to make the crossing from Southampton to New York in less than a week's time.

In a feat never before attempted, the two nearly 900-foot-long leviathans would be built side by side in the Belfast yard, beneath a specially constructed gantry rising to the astonishing height of 220 feet. The original plans called for three funnels, but one more was added, a dummy mainly for appearance (although put to use as a galley flue). The decision was both aesthetic and symbolic. The two successful new Cunarders were

Queen's Island, Belfast.

WHITE STAR TRIPLE-SCREW STEAMERS
"OLYMPIC,"
45000 TONS. AND
"TITANIC,"
45000 TONS.
THE LARGEST STEAMERS IN THE WORLD

Opposite: *With the Olympic's hull nearing completion, the leviathan's true size became apparent.*
Above: *The Olympic and Titanic take shape beneath their huge construction gantry.*
Below: *The Olympic slipped down ways that had been lubricated with more than twenty tons of soap and tallow. Three heavy anchors and more than 80 tons of chain cable were needed to slow the ship to a standstill from its maximum speed of 12.5 knots.*

four-stackers, as were most of the leading ships of the era. Before World War I, four funnels seemed the undisputed badge of power and importance—and safety.

The keel of the *Olympic* was laid down in December 1908. Three months later work commenced on the *Titanic*. Over the next two years, while the *Lusitania* and the *Mauretania* continued breaking each other's speed records, the two huge hulls took shape. By the time the *Olympic*'s 24,600-ton hull slipped down the ways on October 20, 1910, before a select list of invited guests and a huge throng of local onlookers, the full bulk of her sister was already evident. The *Titanic* would come in at a slightly higher gross tonnage, but was virtually identical in most respects. For now all eyes were on the *Olympic* and would stay there for the next year and half. Only tragedy brought the *Titanic* into the foreground.

In every respect the *Olympic* claimed to be superlative, the biggest and most luxurious ship yet built, so big in fact that the channel in Southampton had to be dredged out to accommodate her draft and the pier in New York extended because of her length. Company publicists boasted interminably about her fittings, especially the appointments in first class. Though in some ways less opulent than those of her German competitors, these were impressive, particularly the vast dining saloon, the largest room afloat, and its cavernous reception room, fully half the size of the dining room it led to. Following the Edwardian norm, the first-class smoking room on the *Olympic* remained a preserve of male privilege, here dwarfing the reading and writing room reserved for the women. (On German ships, men and women mixed after dinner in a large lounge.) As on the *Lusitania* and the *Mauretania*, there were elevators, but one of these four lifts was for the exclusive use of travelers in second class, an unprecedented luxury for the less-than superrich. First-class amenities included a Turkish bath staffed by a trained masseuse and an exercise room equipped with all the latest gadgetry. And for the first time on a British ship, there would be a separately operated à la carte restaurant in shameless imitation of the fashionable Ritz-Carlton restaurant on HAPAG's *Amerika*.

Yet for all her 45,324 gross tons, the *Olympic* remained a sleek and comely vessel, barely wider than Cunard's Blue Riband holders while almost a hundred feet longer. According to John Maxtone-Graham, she was, "in the same (Continued on page 81)

Above and left: *The Olympic's and the Titanic's clubby smoking rooms were male-only preserves. According to* The Shipbuilder, *Olympic's was "without doubt the finest apartment of its kind on the ocean."*
Opposite above: *After taking a Turkish bath, first-class passengers could lounge in a cooling room decorated in "the Arabian style of the seventeenth century."*
Opposite below left: *The reception room for the first-class dining saloon.*
Opposite below right: *The Verandah and Palm Court.*

THE FIRST CLASS RECEPTION ROOM.

THE VERANDAH CAFÉ.

breathtaking instance, the last of the lean, yachtlike racers and the first 'floating palace.'" And when she completed her acceptance trials in the spring of 1911 it was clear that she was a good deal faster than her designed 21 knots. Indeed, all portents promised great success as she prepared for her maiden voyage.

Despite a coal strike in Southampton, the *Olympic*'s first ocean crossing began as scheduled on June 14, 1911, with 1,313 passengers on board, including the requisite aristocrats and plutocrats in her plum first-class suites. In command was White Star's senior commander, Captain Edward J. Smith. During the *Olympic*'s uneventful first passage, Bruce Ismay wandered the ship, eavesdropping on the passengers and taking notes of the ship's few deficiencies. Cigar holders were needed in the first-class washrooms and the beds were too springy, uncomfortably exaggerating the vibration from the ship's engines. His only major suggestion, however, was that first-class cabins be added on B deck, taking up an open space the passengers hardly used. When the *Titanic* was completed, these additional cabins, two suites with private promenade decks, two new cabins on A deck, an enclosed forward promenade deck and a restaurant adjunct called the Café Parisien would be the only significant differences between her interior spaces and the *Olympic*'s. When the *Olympic* reached New York and tied up at the newly lengthened but still inadequate Pier 59,

Opposite: *The Olympic heads into the setting sun on her maiden voyage to New York.*
Above: *Lord Pirrie (left) joins Captain Smith on board the* Olympic.

White Star's managing director had reason to be well pleased. She had performed almost flawlessly, averaging 21.7 knots. Ismay jubilantly cabled Lord Pirrie in Belfast: "Olympic is a marvel, and has given unbounded satisfaction."

And she continued to do so until September 20, as she began her fifth voyage to New York. Just after noon, the *Olympic* emerged from Southampton Water and made the usual turn into Spithead, the passage between the Isle of Wight and the mainland that led to the English Channel and her first stop, the French port of Cherbourg. As she did so, the Royal Navy cruiser HMS *Hawke*, having just rounded Egypt Point on the Isle of Wight, entered the same channel on a converging course. Exactly what happened next was never settled. Either the *Olympic* overtook the *Hawke* or the *Hawke* overtook the *Olympic*. But the final result was not open to debate. When the *Hawke*'s bow came alongside the *Olympic*'s starboard side, the warship began to be drawn helplessly toward the huge passenger liner. All attempts to counter the apparent suction proved fruitless, and the *Hawke* smashed into the *Olympic*'s starboard quarter, nearly capsizing before she spun away, "like a top," in the words of her commander.

Both ships sustained serious damage. Only the hasty rigging of collision mats prevented the *Hawke* from sinking. The *Olympic* had a gaping hole in her shell plating above the waterline and a serious puncture under water, a damaged starboard propeller shaft and nicked blades on her starboard propeller. Unable to continue to New York, she disembarked her passengers, who had to resume their journeys on other ships. After temporary repairs, the *Olympic* returned to Belfast for extensive work on her hull and a new propeller shaft, which was commandeered from the still-building *Titanic*, delaying her completion.

The collision with the *Hawke* caused many to ask whether ocean liners had grown beyond the point of safety. (On the *Olympic*'s first arrival in New York, a tug had been sucked in under her stern, only scraping some paint off the *Olympic*'s hull but suffering serious damage itself.) Yet bigger ships were already in the works. The new ships of HAPAG's *Imperator* class would be over fifty thousand gross tons and Cunard was reportedly planning a sixty-thousand-ton behemoth. None other than Lord Pirrie had recently mused that a hundred-thousand-ton ocean liner seemed perfectly possible, even desirable. Certainly the main risk seemed to be to smaller vessels that got too close to these giants. And later that year, when the *Olympic* returned to service, she had lost none of her popularity.

In all, Smith commanded the *Olympic* on nine voyages to New York and back before relinquishing the captain's chair to assume command of the *Olympic*'s younger sister. The *Titanic*'s maiden voyage would be his swansong. After the brand-new ship's

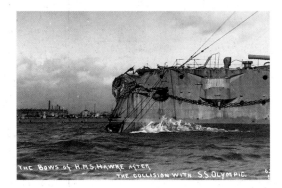

Above: HMS Hawke *before and after her nearly fatal collision with the* Olympic. *Her crushed bow indicates just how close she came to sinking.* **Opposite:** *Crewmen peer out from the huge triangular gash in the* Olympic's *starboard quarter left by the* Hawke. *Fortunately, second-class passengers who might otherwise have been in their staterooms were eating lunch when the collision happened.*

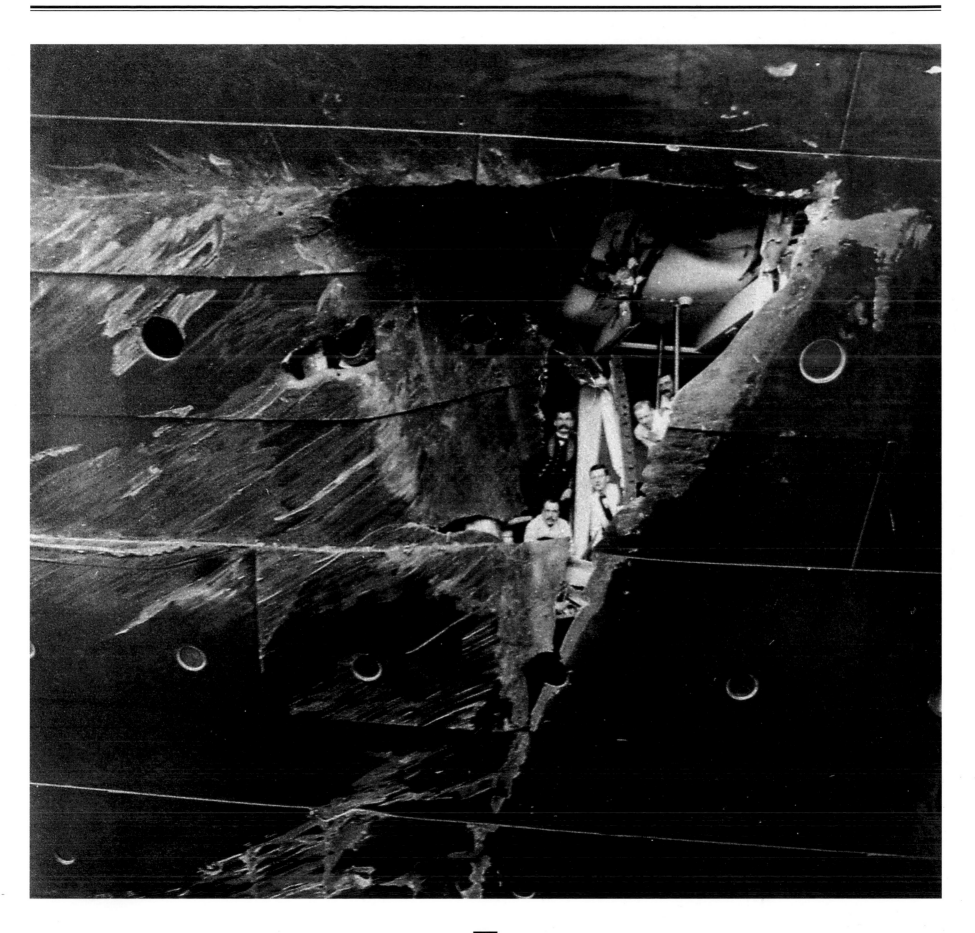

return from New York, Smith planned to retire in glory as White Star's commodore and the beloved "millionaire's captain," who consorted as easily with American financiers and English gentry as he did with the officers on his bridge.

The departure of the *Titanic* on April 10, 1912, on her maiden voyage, made minor ripples compared with the *Olympic*'s inaugural trip less than a year earlier. In Southampton a big crowd saw her off, but there were no ceremonies and no long-winded speeches from local dignitaries and invited bigwigs. Her first-class passenger list, however, which included John Jacob Astor, one of America's wealthiest men, was

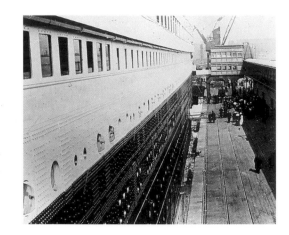

Left: *The Titanic sits pierside in Southampton on the morning of her maiden voyage.*
Below: *On her own at last, the largest moving object the world had ever seen steams past Ireland's Old Head of Kinsale on Thursday April 11, 1912.*
Overleaf: *Late on Sunday April 14, the Titanic enters the ice field.*

remarkable and may well be unsurpassed in the annals of ocean travel. This was the era when wealth equaled celebrity, and the *Titanic's* maiden voyage had clearly attracted an unusual number of the transatlantic elite. In fact, however, her greatest claim to fame seemed likely to be a brief reign as the largest ship in the world. At 882.5 feet, she was identical in length to the *Olympic*, the previous record holder, but the prize for size would soon pass to Hamburg-Amerika's 909-foot-long *Imperator*, due to enter service the following year.

Five days later, without ever having encountered a storm at sea, the *Titanic* had

become the most famous passenger ship in history, a place she retains to this day. And although the story of her wreck has been told countless times, it seems to have lost none of its fascination. This enduring allure stems only partly from the scale of the tragedy—more than 1,500 lives lost, still, with the exception of a 1987 Philippines ferry disaster, the worst death toll from a wreck at sea during peacetime. For the *Titanic* seems to have it all, an irresistible combination of human drama and symbolic *gravitas*.

To many observers, especially proud Britons, she and her sister seemed to represent the final triumph of technology over nature. Although her builders never claimed that the *Titanic* was unsinkable, she was widely believed to be so. Even Captain Smith, who had spent a lifetime on the sea and should have known better, had a few years before remarked of an earlier White Star ship, the *Adriatic*, "I cannot imagine any condition which would cause a ship to founder. I cannot conceive of any vital disaster happening to this vessel. Modern shipbuilding has gone beyond that." Smith was only articulating a widely held sentiment. And the *Titanic* boasted the latest in safety features, most notably watertight compartments whose doors could be closed electrically. So safe were these huge ships considered to be that the British Board of Trade hadn't bothered to revise its lifeboat requirements to reflect the increased numbers carried. There were lifeboats on board for barely one-third the number of passengers and crew when the ship was fully booked. Not that this posed any problem. As the *Republic* had shown, a ship with the *Titanic*'s safety features would surely sink so slowly that help would arrive with time to spare. The lifeboats would be needed only to ferry passengers back and forth.

To technological arrogance, to Edwardian pride that went before a tragic fall, must then be added the element of chance. Somehow the binoculars for the crow's nest had disappeared, possibly stolen or misplaced, so the lookout who peered into Atlantic darkness did so without their aid. What's more, he did so on a most unusual night, with no moonlight to reflect off a floating mountain of ice and a sea so calm no surf would etch a berg's perimeter, the bioluminescence making it visible in time for evasive action. Never in Captain Smith's experience had the ice been so far south this late in the season. And there was one final mischance: when the iceberg was sighted—too late to avoid a collision—the ship might have been saved had the officers on the bridge steered her straight into it rather than turning the wheel. The glancing blow

that ruptured the *Titanic's* hull over a distance of roughly 250 feet and admitted water into six of her compartments sealed her fate.

In retrospect, it is easy to fault the *Titanic's* skipper for not exercising more caution. Having received repeated ice warnings, he did not slow his ship down. But Smith was only doing what he and captains like him had been doing for years, taking calculated risks to make their companies look good. It was a risk no different in kind from the one that had led to the wreck of the *Republic* three years earlier. But Captain Smith's casual, almost cavalier, air that evening, when he lingered late over a second cigar following an elegant dinner with some of the ship's more distinguished passengers, casts him in an inevitably unfavorable light.

Abetting these dramatic elements is the time the ship took to sink, long enough for hundreds of minor dramas to be played out on her ever-more-sloping decks but not long enough for help to arrive. Once the iceberg disappeared back into the cold, clear night, the ship remained afloat for two and a half hours. At first the great liner appeared so slightly damaged that most of the passengers and many in the crew refused to believe she was doomed. (Not so the men in the rapidly filling engine spaces who kept steam up and the lights on almost to the end. Not so Captain Smith, who knew within minutes that his ship was done for.) In the first-class lounge, the band played upbeat tunes, and for a time there was almost a festive air. The first lifeboats left the ship far less than full. The one occupied by Sir Cosmo and Lady Duff Gordon, among the *Titanic's* few titled passengers, rowed off with only twelve on board. Its capacity was forty. Although there were exceptions, the prevailing rule was women and children first. When husbands helped their wives into a boat and waved goodbye, most assumed a speedy reunion.

But soon the slope of the decks became disturbing, and the frisson of a harmless adventure gave way to alarm. Crewmen had to physically prevent passengers from storming the lifeboats. Various survivors reported at least one shot being fired to quell an incipient riot. In a grim echo of the *Republic*, the prerogatives of class superseded common humanity. Until near the end, some of the third-class passengers remained trapped below decks, prevented by locked gates and stern stewards from reaching the boats. And through it all another ship was visible on the horizon, seemingly oblivious to the distress rockets being fired from the stricken liner.

Finally, after the lifeboats had departed and the bow had slipped underwater, the hundreds of people clinging to the upjutting stern faced their mortality. Some jumped, some waited for the ship to rear up and suddenly sink. Few survived more than several minutes in the near-freezing waters. But there were some miraculous escapes. A baker who had spent the evening aiding others while fortifying himself with whisky stepped off the stern as it dropped beneath him and paddled amiably for several hours, apparently insulated against the ice-cold water by all the alcohol he had consumed. Seventeen-year-old Jack Thayer, about to inherit a Philadelphia fortune, leaped from the rail when the water was still twelve or fifteen feet below, then swam as hard as he could. One of the ship's funnels narrowly missed him as it fell, and he was almost drowned by its suction. But when he gasped to the surface, he bumped up against an overturned collapsible lifeboat and was hauled to safety. Of those who watched in wonder and horror as the ship disappeared, he was one of the many who felt sure she had broken in two at the surface.

Top: *Jack Thayer.*
Above: *W. T. Stead.*
Previous page: *At 1:40 p.m.
the* Titanic's *bow had dipped
under the water.*
Right: *By approximately
2:15 p.m. her stern was
high in the air.*

The final moments of the rich and famous became legends. John Jacob Astor asked if he could join his much younger and very pregnant wife in the lifeboat. But when Second Officer Lightoller refused his request, Astor walked politely away, a gentleman to the last. (When his body was recovered, there was more than two thousand dollars in his pocket.) Ida Straus refused to leave her husband, Isidor, one of the owners of Macy's department store. "We have lived together many years," she told him. "Where you go, I go." William T. Stead, the crusading English journalist on his way to speak to a peace conference in New York, was last seen quietly reading in the first-class smoking room.

Top: *Crowds gather outside the*
New York American *waiting for news
of the Titanic's fate.*
Far left: *The front page of the*
New York Times *of April 16, 1912.*
Left: *Survivors crowd onto the fo'c'sle
of the Carpathia as she arrives at her
New York pier.*

The last act of the drama came with the daring rescue by the Cunarder *Carpathia*. Ignoring caution, Captain Arthur Rostron raced through a sea studded with icebergs and arrived on the scene just as dawn was breaking. Meticulous to a fault, he had transformed his passenger ship en route to the Mediterranean into an emergency field hospital by the time the first lifeboats were alongside and the half-dead survivors were being helped on board. "One thing stands out in my mind about it all," he later wrote, "the quietness. There was no noise or hurry. When our passengers at length came on deck they were some time before they seemed to realize the stupendous nature of the tragedy; it was too big to assimilate at once."

Above (top and bottom): Survivors from the Titanic's crew were photographed upon their emotional arrival back in Southampton. Above right: A memorial to the Titanic's engineers was dedicated in Southampton's East Park in April 1914, two years after the sinking.

But assimilated it eventually was. The repercussions of the loss of the *Titanic* were both immediate and lasting. Never again would a ship carry fewer lifeboats than could take away all those on board. Wireless, until now a part-time service on smaller ships, became a twenty-four-hour-a-day necessity. Nor would future captains race brazenly into a field of ice, trusting only the eyesight of their lookouts and the strength and maneuverability of their vessels. Furthermore, they would be required to follow a more southerly summer route, reducing the risk of an iceberg encounter. And information about ice conditions would no longer be left to chance sightings by passing ships radioed at random. Soon the International Ice Patrol, established jointly by the British and the Americans, would monitor the presence of ice in the shipping lanes. *(Continued on page 100)*

Recalling the *Titanic*

A good deal has changed since we explored the wreck of the *Titanic* in the summer of 1986. For example, the crow's nest that we saw still attached to the fallen foremast is now gone. And the foremast itself has now buckled and collapsed farther. As well, more than three thousand artifacts have been lifted from the debris field. But the wreck site retains its essential character. The bow section still sits upright and remarkably intact, its knife edge seeming to plow a furrow in the bottom mud. The stern section still rises above the ocean floor, looking for all the world like a building after a massive internal explosion. These two starkly different faces of death could almost stand for the starkly different fates of those who were saved and those who were drowned.

Top: *With* Alvin *settled gently on the bridge,* Jason Jr. *explores the crow's nest.*
Below left: *The wonderfully preserved telemotor control on the bridge.*
Below right: *Since our 1986 visit, the crow's nest has collapsed.*

Above: *The opened window of first-class stateroom U on the boat deck.*
Below: Alvin *sends* JJ *down the grand staircase.*

Right: *Exploring the boat deck,* JJ *peers into what was once the* Titanic's *first-class gymnasium.*

For all the subsequent attention, little has been added in these past twelve years to our knowledge of the ship or how it sank. The 1987 salvage expedition found the starboard propeller we had missed. The 1991 IMAX filmmaking expedition, brought back images of unprecedented clarity of the wreck. And in 1995 moviemaker James Cameron took the most dramatic video yet of the bow and fo'c'sle, images he planned to use in his *Titanic* feature

movie. Of more interest to me, however, he explored deeper into the ship than anyone before. On its descent down the grand staircase, Cameron sent his tethered robot into the sitting room of the starboard parlor suite, one of the more deluxe first-class accommodations. The robot's eye spotted the ruins of a chair and got a close look at the beautiful brass firebox in the remains of the fireplace. Even more exciting, however, the robot ventured down to

the D-deck reception room outside the first-class dining room. Here it found remains of wood paneling, pillars with pieces of intact woodwork, an octagonal ceiling fixture dangling down and one of the main entry doors through which the first-class passengers boarded the ship. One of the double doors still hangs on its hinges, its ornate iron grillwork clearly visible.

Considerable hullabaloo attended the attempt in the summer of 1996 to raise a piece of the hull from the debris field, but far more interesting was the ultrasound investigation of the area of the bow damaged by the iceberg. These images revealed six small tears or openings affecting the first six compartments. Just as we had surmised in 1986, the great gash was a myth and the actual openings into the ship seem to have been the result of rivets popping and hull plates separating.

Top: *Many cast-iron bench frames like this one have been lifted from the debris field.*
Above left: *This cup, sitting poignantly atop a boiler, is one of the most haunting images we brought back in 1986.*
Above right: *This safe, which is actually missing its back, was dramatically opened during the television special following the first salvage expedition.*
Bottom and right: *Most of the debris trails away from the stern, which lies almost 2,000 feet south of the bow.*

(Continued from page 93)   As for the *Olympic*, her sunny childhood had abruptly been cast into shadow. When the *Titanic* struck the iceberg, the *Olympic* had been outbound from New York, but more than five hundred miles from her sister's distress position. Nonetheless, Captain Herbert Haddock poured on steam and altered course for the sinking ship while on board all entertainments were canceled. But with all those saved embarked on the *Carpathia*, he was able to perform only one sad task. Because his ship was closer to New York, he was in a position to relay the list of survivors to White Star's offices there. This accomplished, he completed the voyage to Southampton, which was already a city in mourning.

Despite the loss of the *Titanic*, White Star proceeded with preparations for the *Olympic*'s next scheduled crossing. In addition to the twenty boats already on board, twenty-four collapsible lifeboats were secured on the boat deck, and the same Board of Trade inspector who had cleared the *Titanic* for departure two weeks earlier pronounced the *Olympic* ready for the voyage. At the last minute, however, the stokehold crew, many of whom had friends or relatives who had died on the *Titanic*, deserted the ship. They distrusted the collapsibles and demanded they be replaced by conventional wooden boats.

This seemingly minor dispute set off a series of delays while the ship lay anchored off Spithead, and the passengers grew increasingly impatient. When a new stokehold crew was drummed up, other members of the ship's company deserted in protest over their inexperience. That led to further delays while a replacement deck crew was mustered. Now two days behind schedule, White Star finally canceled the voyage and took the strikers to court. The company's reputation was at its lowest ebb. And when the *Olympic* finally resumed her regular sailing schedule in mid-May, her passenger complement was below what it should have been for that time of year.

White Star realized that its greatest ship needed more than extra lifeboats to win back the confidence of the traveling public. Accordingly, at the end of the summer of 1912, the *Olympic* was withdrawn from service for a major overhaul that took six months. Her boilers were removed so her double bottom could be extended up the ship's sides to give her hull an inner skin. Five of the bulkheads dividing the ship into watertight compartments were raised to the level of the bridge deck. These invisible

Above: *In the wake of the* Titanic *disaster, additional collapsible lifeboats are loaded on board the* Olympic. **Below:** *Workers install the* Olympic's *inner skin, part of the post-*Titanic *reconstruction that lasted six months.*

WHITE STAR LINE

R.M.S. "OLYMPIC" 46,359 Tons
(The largest British Steamer)

Above: *The Olympic wearing wartime camouflage intended to fool marauding German U-boats.*
Right: *In June 1913, Hamburg-Amerika's* Imperator *became the world's biggest ship. She was joined the next year by the* Vaterland. *But the third in the series, the* Bismarck, *lay incomplete throughout the First World War.*

safety features, combined with the very visible addition of forty-eight lifeboats (for a total of sixty-eight), allowed her owners to boast, "In her will be embodied everything that human foresight has devised for the safety of passengers and crew."

White Star also took the opportunity to make modifications to improve the passenger accommodation. Five additional first-class cabins now graced the promenade deck, the à la carte restaurant was expanded, and a Café Parisien, which had proved so popular on the *Titanic's* maiden voyage, would recreate the illusion of an ocean-going sidewalk café. But the ship that set out for New York on April 2, 1913, on its first voyage of a new year and a new season, would only slowly win back its following against stiff new competition. In June, the first of Hamburg-Amerika's luxurious new passenger giants entered the race. She was the monumental *Imperator*, with a capacity for roughly 5,000 passengers and grandiose first-class accommodations.

Hamburg-Amerika Linie, Hamburg

IMPERATOR

Verzeichnis der Reisenden

Were it not for the advent of war, however, the *Olympic* might have regained her rightful place much sooner. Perhaps she was not as luxurious as the new HAPAG monsters, but she was steadier and more comfortable. The *Imperator* turned out to be top heavy, rolling uncomfortably in a sea and listing noticeably even in calm water. As a result, the pilots who brought her into New York nicknamed her "Limperator."

The *Olympic* would go on to lead a long and successful life in war and peace. One can easily imagine it as the life the *Titanic* might have led. The *Olympic*'s wartime career roughly parallels that of the *Mauretania*—although she never saw service as a hospital ship. During the Gallipoli campaign, she ferried troops to the eastern Mediterranean. Then she became a regular transport carrying Canadian troops between Halifax and Liverpool. When the United States entered the war, she joined the *Mauretania* in bringing the doughboys over. And in one brief moment of glory, she rammed and sank a German U-boat in the English Channel.

In the twenties and thirties, converted to oil and spruced up by yet another interior renovation, the *Olympic* would remain a profitable and fashionable ship, attracting her share of wealth and celebrity. In 1921, Charlie Chaplin chose her for his first return to England since before the war. In 1924 she carried the body of her builder, Lord Pirrie, home from New York to Belfast. Later the same year, she sailed from New York with the dashing young Prince of Wales, the future Edward VIII, on board. (He charmed the passengers and made great use of the squash court.)

The *Olympic* had her share of postwar mishaps, including a collision with a smaller liner while backing away from her New York pier. But the closest echo of the *Titanic* disaster would come very near the end of her life, in 1934, when she sliced through the Nantucket Lightship in a fog, sinking the vessel and ending the lives of seven of the ship's eleven-man crew, although the *Olympic* was barely damaged. The tragedy resulted from the same sort of calculated risk that had led to the *Titanic* disaster twenty-two years before and provided an eerie reminder of the sinking of the *Republic* in 1909. In foggy weather, captains routinely used the lightship's radio signal as a bearing, turning only at the last minute to avoid a collision. A few months earlier, the lightship had been grazed by a passing liner. (Continued on page 106)

Above: The troopship Olympic *at anchor in Halifax harbor, from which she carried thousands of Canadian soldiers to join the war in Europe.*
Left: The Olympic *remained a popular ship during the 1920s, her decks once again crowded with passengers (far left), her regular departures from New York a part of the city's fabric (middle left), and sporting White Star's new logo (left) to help her compete in the postwar world.*
Right: In 1921, Charlie Chaplin sailed to England aboard the Olympic.

Olympic Today

Many of the Olympic's interior fittings and furnishings survive today in England. Left: *The fireplace, the mirror, some paneling and light fixtures from the first-class lounge now decorate the dining room of the White Swan Hotel in Alnwick.*
Above and below: *The first-class lounge then, and one of its oval stained-glass windows today.*
Opposite top: *Light fixtures from the grand staircase (left) and from the first-class smoking room (right).*
Opposite below: *The balustrade from the aft grand staircase in the White Swan Hotel.*

All such happenings great and small lay in the future when a tragedy almost equal to the *Titanic's* unfolded in the fog-shrouded St. Lawrence River in the spring of 1914, only a few months before the outbreak of the Great War. Ironically, had both ships involved exercised less caution, the accident would likely not have happened.

As with the wreck of the *Republic*, the culprit was fog, but a fog peculiar to the St. Lawrence at this time of year, when the warm air of late spring encounters a river chilled by icy meltwater. The two main actors in the drama were the Canadian Pacific steamship *Empress of Ireland*, outbound from Quebec, and the Norwegian collier *Storstad*, steaming upriver and loaded to the waterline. Their stage was a stretch of water just east of Rimouski near the St. Lawrence's south shore, where the river opens up and navigation becomes simpler and safer. The *Empress*, having just dropped her pilot at Father Point, was still quite close to shore. The *Storstad*, about to pick up her pilot for the voyage upriver to Montreal, was hugging the coastline.

The ships sighted each other near 2:00 a.m. on May 29, till then a calm, clear

Above: The Canadian Pacific liner Empress of Ireland was one of the two largest and fastest ships on the Liverpool–Quebec City run.
Below: Captain Henry Kendall strolls the deck with a nattily attired first-class passenger.

Above: *In clement weather, the now-extinct game of deck cricket was enjoyed by the* Empress of Ireland's *passengers.* Below: *The ship's music room, while no match for the public rooms of ships on the New York run, was luxurious nonetheless.*

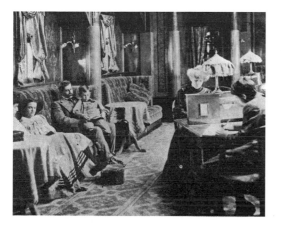

night. On the bridge of the *Empress of Ireland*, Captain Henry Kendall guessed that the approaching ship was roughly eight miles away, giving him ample time to cross her bow before he set his course for more open water. When he judged he was safely beyond the collier's path, he did so. If he held his new course, the two ships should pass starboard side to starboard side, comfortably apart. Moments after he had executed this maneuver, a creeping bank of fog swallowed the Norwegian ship, then the *Empress*.

Although nothing like the *Titanic* in terms of size or elegance, the *Empress of Ireland* was the class of the Liverpool–Quebec City run that linked Canadian Pacific's steamships with its transcontinental railroad. Celebrities on board were few, notably the actor Laurence Irving, famous son of the legendary Henry, and his wife, the actress Mabel Hackney, returning from a successful Canadian tour. They and most of the other passengers, which included roughly 170 members of the Salvation Army heading to a big convention in London, were by this time of night sound asleep. So were most of the crew.

Worried by the fog and the proximity of the other ship, Captain Kendall gave three blasts on his whistle, indicating to the other ship that he was ordering his engines full astern. Soon the 14,191-ton liner had slowed to a crawl, but Kendall kept her bow pointing on the course he had chosen and waited for a clear sign that the other ship was safely past. The next thing he saw were two masthead lights materializing out of the murk to starboard and heading straight at him. The two ships were already too close to avoid a collision, but Kendall ordered a sharp turn to starboard in a vain attempt to swing his stern enough away from the approaching vessel that it would deliver a glancing blow. The impact when it came was deceptively gentle. The *Storstad*'s bow, however, "had gone between the liner's steel ribs as smoothly as an assassin's knife," wrote James Croall in his account of the disaster. And the wound was fatal.

Water poured into the starboard side of the ship so fast that most of the people sleeping in starboard cabins didn't have a chance. There was no time for the prerogatives of class to be tested, beyond the simple reality that residents of the higher-up first-class cabins were more likely to have some chance of survival. As the *Empress of Ireland* listed sharply to starboard, water began rushing into portholes left open despite the rule requiring their closure once a voyage was under way. The list quickly became so extreme that only five or six boats could be successfully launched. After ten minutes, the liner lurched and lay on her side with hundreds of passengers perched on her hull, a situation that momentarily seemed "like sitting on a beach watching the tide come in," according to one survivor. A mere fourteen minutes after the collision, she sank. And by the time the last nearly-frozen survivor had been fished from the water, the death toll was staggering. Of the 1,477 on board, 1,012 lost their lives, including 840 passengers, 8 more than had died when the *Titanic* sank.

What had happened? According to the first mate of the *Storstad*, who didn't rouse his sleeping captain until after all the crucial decisions had been made, he and his colleagues on the bridge had distinctly seen the *Empress of Ireland*'s red navigational light just before the fog closed in. If that were true, that red light meant her port side was showing, which signaled that the big ship had turned to pass them to portside. And this is what the men on the *Storstad*'s bridge assumed. After a few minutes groping blindly forward, the *Storstad*'s mate grew nervous and ordered the collier to turn to

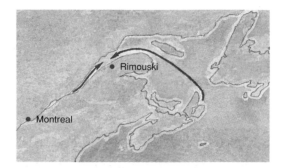

The **Empress of Ireland** *and the* **Storstad** *meet near Rimouski, Quebec.*

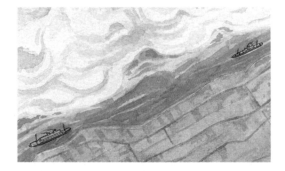

The **Empress** *alters course to port just as the fog rolls in.*

Seeing the **Storstad** *bearing down, Captain Kendall orders a starboard turn.*

The **Storstad's** *bow fatally punctures the* **Empress's** *hull on her starboard side.*

The sinking of the Empress of Ireland *never gained the lasting fame of the* Titanic *disaster, despite the loss of even more passengers. Soon it would be overshadowed by the outbreak of World War I. But it did briefly garner headlines and inspire lurid magazine features around the world. Here, an artist has recreated the final moments of the sinking for Collier's magazine.*

starboard, away from what he now presumed to be the other ship's course. In reality he was turning the *Storstad* directly into the *Empress*'s side.

Captain Kendall, who had been thrown off his bridge when the ship lurched onto its beam ends, swore to his dying day that he had altered course cleanly and maintained it faithfully as the fog closed in. He always blamed Norwegian negligence for the disaster. "You have sunk my ship!" were practically the first words he uttered when he was pulled on board the *Storstad* to encounter her skipper. But perhaps his helmsman had swung her too far before she settled in on her proper course. Perhaps, as one of his crew later testified, there was a problem with the steering that caused his ship to wobble unpredictably on her course. Or perhaps the many lights of the brightly lit passenger vessel confused those on board the *Storstad*. No one will ever know for sure. For certain, fog had once again proved to be a treacherous enemy. Yet had the two ships simply kept their courses and held their speeds, they would have passed each other without incident.

Coming as it did so soon after the sinking of the *Titanic*, the loss of the *Empress of Ireland* underlined the difficulty of building a ship that couldn't sink, even of building

a ship guaranteed to sink so slowly that rescue was inevitable. True the *Storstad* was the worst imaginable ship to have collided with the liner. Her longitudinal bracing, designed to break through ice, made her a lethal weapon; the fact she was fully loaded meant she punctured the *Empress* well below the waterline. (She penetrated the liner to a depth of at least twenty-five feet and left a gaping a hole at least fourteen feet wide.) The *Empress* sank too fast for her safety features to be fully operational. She had enough lifeboats for all her passengers and crew but could not launch them in time. Many of her watertight doors, operated manually, could not be closed with the ship listing sharply and water rushing in.

But despite the scale of the tragedy, it never achieved anything like the *Titanic*'s fame or enduring fascination. The *Empress of Ireland* was not a particularly famous or fashionable ship, and she sank so soon before the outbreak of the war that attention soon shifted to graver matters. The commission of inquiry, chaired by the same Lord Mersey who presided over the hearings into the sinking of both the *Titanic* and the *Lusitania*, was held in Quebec City, far from the international limelight. But the lessons from the *Empress of Ireland*'s demise would have to be relearned barely forty years later during the sinking of the *Andrea Doria*, when once again fog proved more than a match for the latest in seagoing technology.

Above: *Three survivors from the* Empress of Ireland.
Left: *When the* Storstad *pulled into Quebec City, observers could see that her powerful bow had been barely blunted by its impact with the hull of the* Empress.
Opposite top: *Sailors carry coffins of the dead ashore at Canadian Pacific's pier in Quebec City from the Canadian revenue cutter* Lady Grey.
Opposite bottom left: *The crowd gathered outside the pier, awaiting the arrival of the* Lady Grey.
Opposite bottom right: *In a strange echo of the* Titanic *disaster, Lord Mersey presided over the official inquiry into the sinking of the* Empress of Ireland. *(He would later chair the inquiry into the sinking of the* Lusitania.*) Once again, he exonerated those in authority.*

Exploring the *Empress of Ireland*

Today the *Empress of Ireland* lies in about 130 feet of water, well within the reach of scuba divers. But because the St. Lawrence is a frigid thirty-four degrees Fahrenheit even in summer and has tidal currents that run up to five knots and can limit visibility, this is a dive for experts. Nonetheless, the *Empress* has been visited hundreds of times since it was "rediscovered" in the mid-1960s.

Above: *The bow of one of the ship's remaining lifeboats.*
Below left: *A skull in the wreckage.*
Below right: *A remnant of floor tile.*

Some divers have treated the wreck with respect and increased our knowledge of her tragedy; others have left a trail of senseless damage.

Modern divers follow a highway that was blasted into the heart of the ship in the summer of 1914, mere weeks after the disaster. Canadian Pacific hired a salvage company to retrieve the first-class mail, the purser's safe and $150,000 in silver bullion (more than $2 million today). Descending through the explosion hole down to the first-class baggage and mail room, one will encounter a dangerous tangle of wire and an interior debris field of shattered suitcases and their decaying contents.

Although the ship rests on a gravel, sediment-free river bottom, the insides of the *Empress of Ireland* are half-hidden by the silt steadily deposited by the St. Lawrence River over the years. Because the ship rests

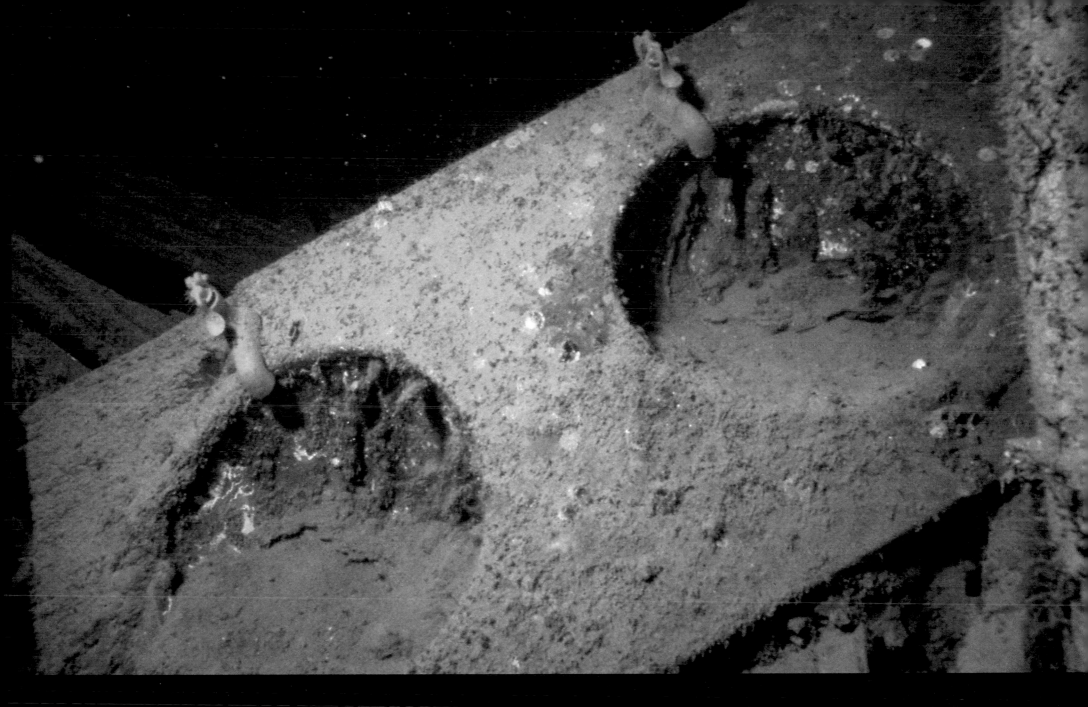

Opposite above left: *These rubble-strewn stairs lie deep inside the ship.*
Opposite top right: *A stack of first-class dishes.*
Opposite middle and bottom right: *The first-class dining saloon in 1914 and one of its round, etched-glass windows as it looks today.*
Above: *Sinks inside one of the ship's washrooms.*

at so sharp an angle, the starboard side of every interior room is buried, along with all the items set loose as the ship sank. In the mail room, one diver discovered a whole box of neatly bundled and tied newspapers, the paper still white, the type still readable, dated May 27, 1914, the day before the ship left port. The next time he returned, the silt had shifted, burying the evidence.

In the ship's dining saloon, oak chairs and tables appear to float in the silt like flotsam and the remains of light fixtures dangle from the steeply angled ceiling. In the adjoining pantry, most of the first-class china that was still in its racks as late as the early 1980s is now gone, as are most other moveable objects in the accessible regions of the wreck, including the ship's bell, one of its propellers, the main bridge telegraph and the telemotor. Sadly, some divers have taken the bones of some of the more than one thousand people who died when the *Empress of Ireland* went down.

Chapter

4

The *Titanic*'s younger sister *Britannic* was to have been the most opulent of the three White Star giants. But World War I caused her conversion into a Spartan hospital ship, in which guise she was sunk by a German mine in the Mediterranean in November 1916.

The death throes of the Britannic, which sank only two miles from the Greek island of Kea on a crystal-clear Mediterranean morning.

Forgotten Sister

The Brief Life of
White Star's Britannic,
1914 ~ 1916

WHITE STAR LINE R.M.S. BRITANNIC - 50,000 TONS-ON THE STOCKS

WHITE STAR LINE R.M.S. "BRITANNIC" - 50,000 TONS-LEAVIN

BRITANNIC

F or Nurse Sheila Macbeth, the sixth voyage of His Majesty's Hospital Ship *Britannic*, on November 12, 1916, began as both a homecoming and a kind of holiday before the real work ahead. "Such a relief to find the same cabin and room-mate," wrote the unmarried, twenty-six-year-old Scot in her diary, "and to see how homely it is now looking, with my chintz cushions and our nice jar of brown beech leaves. Everything is much nicer on this voyage—as there are no passengers (these were always medical officers and nurses—going out to different hospitals in India, Egypt, Salonica or Malta . . .) and in consequence we are allowed to wander all over the ship, and do not find the deck roped off at every turn with a notice saying: 'Officers Only' or 'Passengers Only.' "

Nurse Macbeth's wanderings must have been fascinating, since the ship she was traveling on was the *Titanic*'s younger sister. Only the outbreak of war had prevented the *Britannic* from joining White

By November 1916, the Britannic was showing the wear of wartime service, having made five voyages to carry wounded home from the Mediterranean theater.

White Star planned to make the Britannic even more beautiful than her two older sisters as shown in this drawing of her restaurant's reception room (above).

Middle left: The expanded à la carte restaurant.

Right: Rumor has it that the grand staircase was to be graced by a huge pipe organ.

Left: A booklet commemorating Britannic's launch on February 26, 1914.

WHITE STAR LINE.

ROYAL
AND
UNITED STATES
Mail Steamer
"BRITANNIC"
(TRIPLE SCREW)

LAUNCHED AT BELFAST
26th February 1914.

Reportedly, White Star originally planned to name the new ship the Gigantic, *but the loss of the* Titanic *caused the company to reconsider. The new choice was deliberate. White Star's earlier* Britannic *had been a popular and successful ship and the new name may also have been chosen to appeal to patriotic sentiment with war looming.*

Star's fleet as the largest, the most luxurious—and the safest—passenger ship flying the British flag. Instead her fancy fittings sat in storage, her promenade decks were crowded with hospital beds and her first-class dining room had become the intensive care ward where the most seriously wounded would stay before and after surgery in the operating theater next door, formerly the grand reception room. The public rooms on the upper decks housed the majority of the wounded—close to the boats should they need to abandon ship. The first-class staterooms provided accommodation for the hospital elite—the doctors, the nursing matron, the medical corps officers and the chaplains—while the lesser nurses and orderlies made do with cabins originally intended for lower classes.

The ship's surgeon, Dr. J. C. H. Beaumont, called her "the most wonderful hospital ship that ever sailed the seas." And she was indeed an amazing floating infirmary. With every hospital bed full, the *Britannic* could transport 3,309 patients. Only the *Aquitania* could carry more: almost 4,200 wounded. But until the *Britannic* reached the port of Mudros on the Aegean island of Lemnos, the gathering point for casualties from all the Mediterranean theaters, she would be relatively empty, her nurses, doctors and orderlies with nothing to do except to make sure the hospital was ready to receive its patients. Nurse Macbeth spent much of the first leg of the trip making beds, but still found time each day for a morning gymnastics class given by one of the sergeants and an afternoon swim in the first-class swimming pool, followed by tea and then perhaps a game of cricket out on deck.

It was a pleasant enough interlude before what would be the very serious business of tending victims of a conflict that had long since lost any aura of romance and adventure. By November 1916, the war that was to be "over by Christmas" of 1914 looked as if it might last forever. On the Eastern and Western Fronts, the opposing troops were locked in bloody stalemate. The recent Battle of Jutland, the greatest naval engagement ever, had failed to break the British naval blockade of Europe, increasing pressure on the Germans to resort to unrestricted submarine warfare, despite the risk it might draw the United States into the war. And while the Allies had finally abandoned Gallipoli the previous January, hundreds of thousands of troops were now tied up in Greek Macedonia, Palestine and Mesopotamia, making hospital ships in the

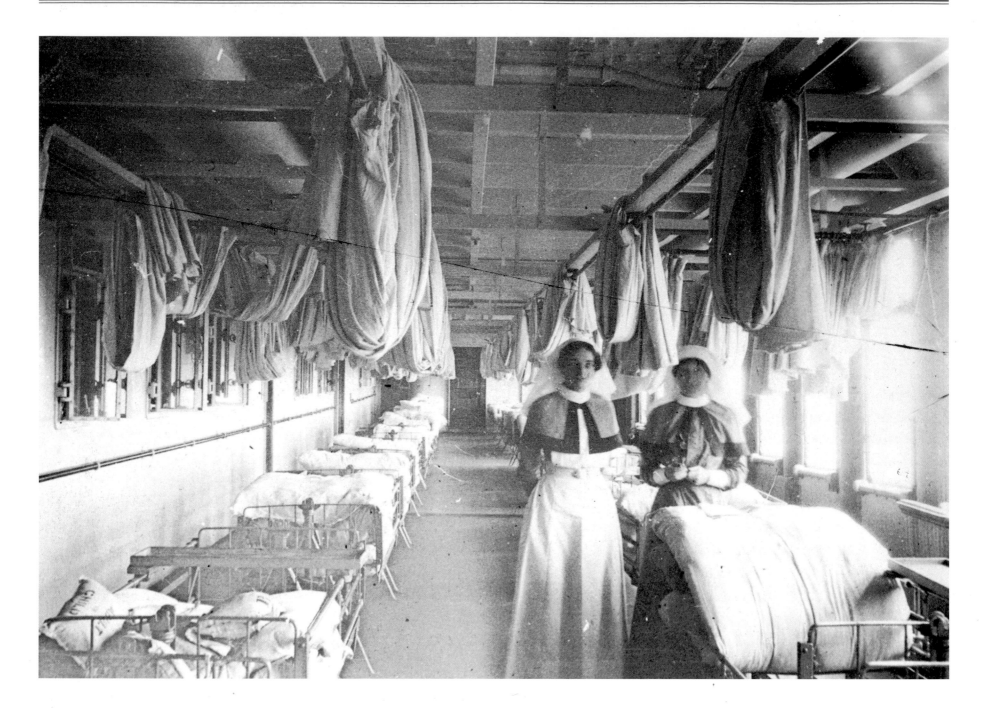

Mediterranean as vital as ever. On the *Britannic*'s most recent trip she had returned with almost every bed full, and it had taken fifteen hospital trains to transport the casualties from Southampton.

In theory, the *Britannic* had nothing to fear from enemy submarines. As a hospital ship she was protected from attack under the Geneva Convention, but this was never a guarantee. The Germans suspected hospital ships of secretly transporting troops—a charge that would be laid against the *Britannic* after she sank. (No evidence to support this charge has ever appeared.) And while the majority of German submarines were occupied in trying to break Britain's Atlantic blockade, a number were active in the Mediterranean, laying mines along routes heavily traveled by troopships and torpedoing enemy targets when the opportunity arose.

Mines, of course, did not distinguish between warships and noncombatants. The many narrow sea passages along the main Mediterranean shipping routes were natural areas for mine laying. And at least one mine-laying submarine had recently been active along the course the *Britannic* would soon be following. This was *U-73*, under the command of Kapitänleutnant Gustav Siess. Late in October, he had been scouting out the Kea Channel between the Greek mainland and the island of Kea just east of Athens. Noting that most ships passed close to the island, he laid two barriers of six mines each at right angles to the shipping lane.

Opposite above: The Britannic's enclosed promenade decks were converted to airy hospital wards
Opposite below left: Belowdecks the hospital quarters were more cramped.
Opposite below middle: Bedridden patients in one of the Britannic's wards pose for the camera.
Opposite below right: Nurse Sheila Macbeth (right) poses on the unfinished grand staircase with two of her colleagues.
Right: U-73, the mine-laying German submarine that almost certainly planted the explosive that sank the Britannic.

Despite these dangers, those traveling aboard the *Britannic* had reason to feel confident. At a service speed of 21 knots—faster if necessary—she could outrun any U-boat. And her builders had designed her to withstand the sort of disaster that had sunk the *Titanic*. A watertight inner skin, running for almost two-thirds of the ship's length and making her eighteen inches wider than her two predecessors, protected her engines and boiler rooms. Five of her seventeen watertight bulkheads extended as high as B deck, also known as the bridge deck, fully forty feet above the waterline. The rest rose as high as E deck. All the bulkheads had the latest in electrically operated watertight doors, and the pumping system allowed any watertight compartment to be drained by means of a valve placed well above the waterline. The higher bulkheads were meant to keep her afloat with any six of her compartments flooded. In theory it would take more than one torpedo to sink her.

And in the unlikely event that she sank, there would be a lifeboat seat for everyone. No one admiring the *Britannic*'s massive profile could doubt that lifeboats had become a priority. Five sets of huge gantry davits towered over the boat deck, while two more graced the poop deck, each responsible for launching six of the largest lifeboats ever carried on a ship and, where a funnel did not block the way, capable of reaching across the superstructure to pick up boats from the other side of the ship if it became impossible to launch them there. (The original plans called for eight of these new davits, but the Admiralty needed the ship before all could be installed; instead, smaller Welin davits like those used on the *Titanic* made up the difference.) Each new gantry davit was powered by a special auxiliary electric motor and had its own electric illumination to facilitate nighttime loading. (As an added benefit, this new lifeboat arrangement opened up space on the boat deck for the use of passengers, a feature that would help make the *Britannic* more attractive when she finally entered commercial service after the war.)

Britannic had one further safety feature in her skipper, Captain Charles Bartlett. A White Star veteran, Bartlett had a reputation for caution. According to his daughter, he was known among his peers as "Iceberg Charlie" because of his ability to "smell" an iceberg and his willingness to travel long distances to avoid it. He also knew his ship and her safety features intimately, having kept a watchful eye on the ship's construction in his prewar role as the company's marine superintendent at Belfast. At the outbreak of the conflict he had undertaken patrolling duties in the North Sea and so was no stranger to the hazards presented by the increasingly aggressive German U-boat fleet.

Five days out of Southampton, on November 17, the *Britannic* arrived at Naples for coaling. This was the standard practice for hospital ships, which wanted their stokeholds full so they could make a nonstop dash home with their cargo of wounded. Mudros was less than a two-day sail from Naples.

Sheila Macbeth and seven of her friends took advantage of the stopover to make an excursion into the Italian countryside with a guide in two rented cars. The trip quickly veered toward slapstick—the tires were full of holes and the cars kept breaking down—but nothing seems to have dampened this woman's youthful high spirits and infectious good humor. The highlight of the day was "lunch at a little country inn—where I could not eat for watching the natives shoveling in spaghetti by the yard—a wonderful sight!" Back in Naples, she did some Christmas shopping.

By evening, the refueling had been completed, but bad weather kept the ship at the wharf for two more days, riding out the storm with the help of her three huge bow anchors. On Sunday evening, the nineteenth, Captain Bartlett took advantage of a break in the weather to set sail, but the storm picked up again and during the night the ship fought her way south through the Bay of Naples. Monday morning found the *Britannic* in calmer weather, steaming through the picturesque Straits of Messina, always Nurse Macbeth's "favorite bit of the voyage."

Anyone watching from the shore as the great ship passed through those famous narrows between the "toe" of Italy and the island of Sicily, would have seen an impressive

Opposite top: The Britannic's watertight doors could be closed automatically to create seventeen compartments, five of them extending up to B deck, three decks higher than on the Olympic *and the* Titanic.
Opposite middle: The Britannic's high gantry davits could each launch six lifeboats.
Opposite bottom: The Britannic's gig being lowered for shore leave in Naples harbor.
Right: Captain Charles Bartlett, whose nickname was Iceberg Charlie.

sight. Four buff-colored funnels towered over a white-painted hull bisected lengthwise by a broad green stripe that ran from bow to stern, interrupted by three huge red crosses. Two more giant crosses affixed to the superstructure were lit at night when the promenade deck was outlined by a line of green lights. Whether the ship was more beautiful by day or darkness was debatable. Her nighttime appearance so impressed the Presbyterian chaplain, Reverend John A. Fleming, that he later described her as like "a picture from fairyland." Day or night, however, there was no mistaking the *Britannic* for anything but a hospital ship.

All hands were busy that Monday in final preparations. "From breakfast time until our afternoon swim, we worked like factory hands," wrote Sheila Macbeth, "tying up all the kits for the next evening so that we might rest the day before the patients came on board." But there was still the time for her cherished afternoon swim. Tuesday promised to be one final holiday before the hard and often gruesome work ahead. That night the ship's company gathered in the main mess hall for the daily church service, "the best since the boat had been in commission," according to Private Percy Tyler of the medical corps, closing with the singing of the familiar hymn, "There Is a Green Hill."

Tuesday morning dawned as perfect a day as November in the Mediterranean can offer. Reverend Fleming rose early to observe "the quietest and loveliest sunrise of the voyage" as the ship followed her easterly course across the mouth of the Gulf of Athens. "The waters were as glass, and the sun shone on them with dazzling brilliance." The long morning light caught the windmills and varied hues of a closely packed Greek village "built high up the steep side of an island, hiding itself cozily between two shoulders of the hill," and he became completely absorbed in the play of light and color, losing all track of time.

By 8:00 a.m. the orderlies of the army medical corps had finished breakfast in their mess, located aft on C deck, and returned to their quarters in the stern, but the nurses, sea scouts and officers were still tucking in to their morning fare in the dining room, almost certainly the space intended for the third-class dining room on F deck. (The sea scouts were sea-going boy scouts who performed mostly menial jobs, such as operating the elevators and carrying messages.) From the boiler rooms and engine rooms to the bridge, meanwhile, a watch change was under way and most of the watertight doors

The Reverend John A. Fleming, the ship's Presbyterian chaplain, left one of the fullest accounts of the Britannic's final morning. But he also described his delight at exploring the impressive ship from stem to stern. "The engines were perhaps the most impressing [sic] thing in the ship," he wrote. "One of the junior engineers, who delighted in showing us round, told us that in the engine-rooms of the Britannic there was more power than in the whole of Birkenhead."

were open to allow for the crew transfer. Just before the watch changed, Captain Bartlett had ordered a course alteration, turning the ship northeast on a line that would take her through the Kea Channel. As he surveyed the glorious morning scene from the bridge, his mind must already have been projecting forward to a midafternoon arrival at Mudros. No sixth sense warned Iceberg Charlie that his peace of mind was about to be shattered.

Nurse Macbeth had slept a trifle late and, having just settled into her place in the dining room, "only managed to get two spoonfuls of porridge before: Bang! and a shiver right down the length of the ship." Reverend Fleming, having finally torn himself away from the passing scene, was leaving his cabin "when there was a great crash, as if a score of plate-glass windows had been smashed together; the great ship shuddered for a moment from end to end." Private Percy Tyler was back in number 2 barrack room following breakfast, cleaning the buttons on his uniform, "when there was a violent bump, which sent me forward a few paces and back again, then the boat regularly danced." None of his mates took the bump seriously, some joking that they were very sorry for the boat the ship had run into.

If the seriousness of the situation was not yet clear to those amidships or farther aft, the very few men who happened to be near the bow at this hour instantly knew the *Britannic* was in deep trouble. They felt a violent explosion, then water began pouring into the ship, washing one man from his quarters on G deck all the way up to E deck. Another barely outraced the flood, making it through a watertight door just before it closed. But miraculously, although an area of the forward part of the ship was in ruins, no one seems to have been killed or even seriously injured in the explosion.

On the *Britannic*'s bridge, Captain Bartlett assumed the ship had struck a mine on the starboard bow. Neither he nor any lookouts had spotted a torpedo track, which should have been obvious on such a calm, clear day. But he reacted coolly and on the assumption that he could still save the ship, ordering the watertight doors closed and requesting an immediate damage report. He had felt only one explosion, so surely the flooding could be contained in the forward compartments. But he was taking no chances. Via the pneumatic tube that linked the bridge to the radio room—another post-*Titanic* safety improvement—he directed the radio operator to send out an immediate distress call. Then he ordered the crew to uncover the boats and that the ship's siren sound the general alarm.

In the dining room, Major Harold Priestly had taken charge of the situation, ordering everyone to remain seated and to go on eating their breakfasts. But the suspense killed every appetite. According to Nurse Macbeth, "there was only a most unnatural silence." Only when the siren sounded did Priestly give the nurses, sea scouts and junior officers permission to leave, but under his watchful eye the evacuation was quiet and orderly.

Sheila Macbeth made straight for her cabin, where she grabbed a coat and her eiderdown pillow and put on her life belt. But she left her dispatch box, which

Opposite above: The hospital camp at Mudros on the island of Lemnos, where the Britannic was heading, consisted of wooden bungalows.
Opposite below: The Britannic at anchor in the harbor at Mudros on an earlier visit to pick up wounded.
Above: Major Harold Priestly of the RAMC took a leading role in organizing the orderly evacuation of the ship.

contained most of her "small treasures." And she doesn't seem to have given even a passing thought to the Christmas gifts so recently purchased in Naples. With one last glance at her homely little home away from home, she headed for the boat deck.

There seems to have been no sense of panic as nurses, crewmen and members of the medical corps collected essential belongings and then proceeded to their boat stations. As on the *Titanic*, the engineers remained at their posts. But the most remarkable case of *sang froid* must surely be that of Nurse Violet Jessop, who had been in a couple of tight spots before. She had been a stewardess on the *Olympic* at the time of its nearly disastrous collision with the *Hawke*. The following year, she served in the same capacity on the *Titanic* during its maiden voyage. When she felt the explosion, however, she calmly continued preparing a breakfast tray for a nursing sister too sick to eat in the dining room, even though she had no doubt the ship was in danger. When she reached the ailing nurse's cabin, she first insisted that breakfast be eaten, then helped the woman get dressed and assisted her to an elevator and thence onto the boat deck. Only then did Jessop dash to her own cabin for a few essentials, above all a toothbrush, an item she had sorely missed after being rescued by the *Carpathia* four and a half years earlier. By the time she reached the boat deck this second time, none of the lifeboats had yet left the ship.

During Jessop's odyssey, the *Britannic's* condition worsened from serious to grave. The explosion had occurred on the starboard side of the bow, roughly where the bulkhead separated the second and third cargo holds. But it had also punctured the bulkhead, sealing off the forepeak and had wrecked the watertight doors in the fireman's passage that led aft into boiler room number 6. This meant the forward five compartments of the ship began to rapidly fill with water, including the forwardmost boiler room, boiler room 6.

But Captain Bartlett had given the order to close the watertight doors and the electrically operated mechanism started to shut the door between boiler room 6 and the next boiler room aft, boiler room 5. Being well aft of the point of the explosion, the door should have operated properly, but it failed to close all the way and water poured through. Soon both boiler rooms were flooded and inoperable. Now the ship's first six forward compartments were filling rapidly, in theory the maximum number that could flood for the ship to survive.

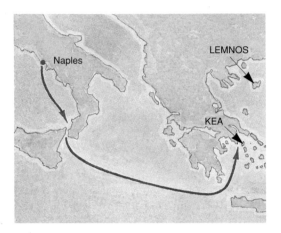

The Britannic's route from Naples to Lemnos took her through the Straits of Messina between Sicily and the "toe" of Italy, across the southern Adriatic, then northward into the Aegean. The ship sank just off the island of Kea, fewer than fifty miles southeast of Athens in only 395 feet of water. For the next sixty years, she lay forgotten and unvisited.

On the morning of Tuesday November 21, 1916, HMHS Britannic *entered the narrow channel between the islands of Kea and Makronisi.*

At 8:12 a.m., the ship struck a single mine, which blasted a hole in the starboard side of the forward hull.

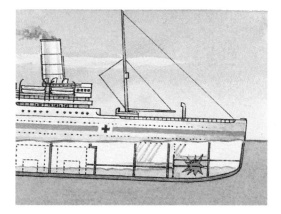

Within minutes the ship was down at the bow and listing to starboard, letting water pour in through open portholes.

The next bulkhead aft, that separating boiler rooms 5 and 4, still held, but the ship soon developed a serious list to starboard, causing the forward portholes on E and F decks to sink beneath the waterline. As on the *Empress of Ireland*, many of these were open—an unconscionable breach of standard safety procedures in a war zone, hospital ship or no—adding to the volume of water flowing into the vessel.

Captain Bartlett now made his one real mistake of the day, thereby increasing the risk for those on board and certainly hastening the sinking. He turned his ship toward the island of Kea, lying tantalizingly close to his position, and ordered the engines full ahead. He desperately hoped to ground the *Britannic* in its shallows, but only succeeded in accelerating the flooding of the forward compartments, increasing the ship's list. Furthermore, as long as the ship was in motion, it was unsafe to lower any of the boats. Quickly realizing he was only making the situation worse, Bartlett ordered the engines stopped.

Before the *Britannic* slowed, two lifeboats left the port side of the ship without permission. These were sucked into the still-turning propellers, which were now just breaking the surface. Violet Jessop was one of those who leaped into the water before the two tiny craft were wrecked, but at first she thought her luck had finally run out. Suction drew her inexorably down. As she struggled upward, her head hit the keel of a wrecked boat and she began to sink again. But a hand reached out and drew her gasping into the air. Eventually she was pulled into another lifeboat, having swallowed seawater but otherwise seeming none the worse for wear. (Only years later did she discover that she had fractured her skull when it hit the bottom of the lifeboat.) Over seventy others, killed or badly wounded, were not so fortunate.

On board the now severely listing *Britannic*, the loading of the remaining boats had been a mostly orderly affair. The nurses and the army corps orderlies assembled on the promenade deck and quietly awaited their turn. Matron E. A. Dowse, a veteran of the Boer War, oversaw the female evacuation with military precision, waiting until every single one of her charges was off the ship before seeing to her own safety. Major Priestly, who had taken charge of the orderlies, kept his troops in line, only allowing fifty men up on the boat deck at any one time.

Only a few elements of the ship's crew exhibited any lack of discipline. A group of firemen commandeered one of the boats on the poop deck and rowed it away half empty, but were persuaded to return to pick up swimmers from the water. A small phalanx of seamen and stewards rushed to port side boats that had just been swung out, but an officer managed to calm them down and restore order. Perhaps these lapses can be blamed on the less-seasoned crews that manned merchant ships in wartime. Whatever the reason, many of the lifeboats left the *Britannic* without any seamen to steer or row them. In Sheila Macbeth's boat, several nurses took the oars. It would seem that the ship's officers overseeing the loading and launching fell down on their responsibilities.

One way or another, however, the ship was soon all but empty, her bow completely underwater, her starboard list increasing and her propellers slowly turning in thin air. Major Priestly took one last turn around the deck then joined the ship's purser in the final boat to leave. The purser carried a precious cargo, the ship's log. The chief engineer and the crew that had remained with him to the last escaped through the funnel casing of the dummy fourth stack, actually a ventilator shaft for the reciprocating engine room, and jumped into the water. Captain Bartlett, who stayed on the bridge to the last, directing the evacuation with a megaphone, sounded the final order to abandon ship—one long blast on the ship's whistle—then stepped off the starboard bridge wing into the water.

From crowded lifeboats or paddling in the cool Aegean, more than a thousand people watched their ship's last moments. Under a perfect blue sky with land so achingly close, the scene took on a surreal quality. Hauling himself into an empty collapsible boat, Captain Bartlett stood alone and watched his command disappear.

Reverend Fleming, who had left in the second-last boat, described the final plunge. "Gradually the waters licked up and up the decks—the furnaces belching forth volumes of smoke, as if the great engines were in their last death agony; one by one the monster funnels melted away as wax before a flame, and crashed upon the decks, till the waters rushed down; then report after report rang over the sea, telling of the explosions of the boilers. The waters moved over the deck still, the bows of the ship dipping deeper and deeper into the sea, until the rudder stood straight up from the surface of the water, and, poised thus for a few moments, dived perpendicularly into the depths, leaving hardly a ripple behind. A sense of the desert overwhelmed my soul."

However evocative, Reverend Fleming's description is inaccurate in at least one

Above: *Among the Royal Navy vessels that raced to the Britannic's rescue were the auxiliary cruiser HMS Heroic (top), and the G-class destroyers* Foxhound *(middle) and* Scourge *(bottom). Along with a Greek fishing boat that arrived quickly on the scene, these ships rescued 1,036 of the 1,066 men and women on board.*

Sheila Macbeth as she looked at the time of the Britannic's final voyage. In 1976 at age 86, she returned to the sinking site at the invitation of Jacques Cousteau. On the third of three attempts in Cousteau's diving saucer, the former nurse finally got another look at the ship that had been her home for a few months during World War I.

important detail. The *Britannic* sank in only 395 feet of water, a depth less than half her length. Therefore the ship could not have reached a perpendicular before it made its final plunge.

The time was 9:07 a.m., roughly fifty-five minutes after the single deadly explosion that had interrupted a routine morning. In less than an hour, the largest British-built ship afloat had vanished, leaving behind thirty-five lifeboats and a scattering of flotsam on an empty sea.

Fortunately, help was close at hand. The auxiliary cruiser *Heroic*, the first of several British warships that responded to the *Britannic's* distress call, soon arrived on the scene, as did a Greek fishing boat from nearby Port St. Nikolo. Both began picking up survivors. The destroyer *Scourge* arrived only minutes later. The destroyer *Foxhound* turned up just before noon, in time to relieve the first two ships, now full to overflowing.

To Sheila Macbeth, it seemed like hours before she was rescued by the *Scourge*, although it must have been much less. The destroyer took on a total of 339 survivors before turning toward Piraeus. Already the sinking seemed a distant fact. "The sailors seemed very pleased to speak to their country-women again," she wrote, "as they had not been home since War began and are never allowed on land. They gave us all the food they had—tea, dog biscuits and oranges out of sacks. Several of them gave us their cap ribbons as souvenirs."

By nightfall most of the survivors had been safely distributed among the British and French ships lying anchored in the Bay of Salamis; the nurses and most of the officers were put up in two local hotels. And when the final accounting of lost and saved was done, the result seemed little short of miraculous. Of the more than one thousand on board, only thirty had died, most of them passengers in the two boats dashed to pieces by the ship's propellers. Had the explosion occurred at any time other than breakfast, the casualty list would likely have been much longer. Had the sinking occurred on the homeward trip from Mudros, with more than three thousand sick and wounded on board, it would have been a *Titanic*-scale catastrophe.

The subsequent naval inquiry, conducted in haste over the next couple of days, shed little light on the sinking or how it could have been avoided. The limited evidence seemed to suggest that in all probability, the ship had not been sunk by a deliberate

German act of aggression. "The effects of the explosion might have been due to either a mine or a torpedo," the report concluded. "The probability seems to be a mine."

On the more vexing question of why a ship designed to float with up to six compartments flooded had sunk—and sunk so quickly—when only her first five bulkheads had been compromised, the inquiry report drew no conclusions, but noted that open portholes had contributed to the volume of water entering the ship. Lesser vessels had survived a single mine or torpedo. The *Britannic*'s sister ship the *Titanic*, which suffered analogous damage along her starboard bow, took more than twice as long to sink. Was there an act of sabotage or an accidental secondary explosion, caused by a contraband cargo of munitions, or perhaps the ignition of highly inflammable ether among the ship's medical supplies? There was no concrete evidence to support any of these theories. Perhaps the open portholes made the fatal difference.

As for the survivors, most of the men faced a far more arduous journey home than any could have imagined, transferred from ship to shore to ship and finally offloaded at Marseilles. From there they traveled for forty hours with little or no food in unheated train carriages to Le Havre, and thence to England. Sheila Macbeth and her fellow nurses fared somewhat better, biding their time on Malta until a hospital ship could take them home. They arrived just after Christmas, more than a month after the sinking. Most quickly and most comfortably home was Captain Bartlett, whose status earned him a seat in a scheduled train from Marseilles. He turned up on his doorstep wearing a Greek suit and Greek shoes he had acquired to replace his ruined uniform.

After a brief outcry in the English papers, the *Britannic* was all but forgotten. For the next sixty years the *Britannic* lay undisturbed in shallow water off the shore of an unimportant Greek island. Although the largest ship to sink during World War I, she left no clear cause for outrage, as had the *Lusitania*, no legacy of tragic symbolism, as had the *Titanic*. It appeared she had been sunk by bad luck, not by an act of deliberate enemy immorality. Most of those on board had survived.

She was sorely missed by those who had sailed on her and by the wounded soldiers waiting for her at Mudros, but other ships filled the void. Only a few liner buffs remembered her and wondered what her life might have been as the *Olympic*'s even grander sister, joining her on the transatlantic run during the roaring twenties and dirty thirties.

Surviving Britannic *crewmembers are shown gathered on the bow of the battleship HMS* Lord Nelson *off Salonika.*

Exploring the *Britannic*

I n the almost eighty years since its sinking, ours was only the second expedition to explore the wreck of HMHS *Britannic*, but the first to see her clearly. Jacques Cousteau visited the wreck in 1976, but—not surprisingly, given the relatively primitive state of underwater cameras then—the images he brought back provided murky evidence of the ship's condition. The *Britannic* seemed to be in one piece, but he thought he'd found evidence of a major secondary explosion that had blasted a huge hole in the forward part of the hull. He also believed the bow had been twisted up at right angles to the hull, so that it jutted toward the surface.

Our plan in late August 1995 was to survey the wreck with the help of the navy's nuclear-powered *NR-1* submarine, small by navy sub standards but far more spacious and comfortable than the research submersibles I'm accustomed to. (You can actually stand up!) Once we had a clear picture of the layout of the wreck site, we would take still and video footage of the ship with our two remotely operated vehicles (ROVs), *Voyager* (provided by Perry Tritech, Ltd.) and *Phantom* (provided by the University of Connecticut's National Undersea Research Program). Using *NR-1* primarily as a second light source, *Voyager* was hooked up to a 3-D imaging system that allowed those of us in the control room to feel as though we could reach out and

Top: *Our 1995 research vessel,* Carolyn Chouest, *rides the calm Aegean just off the island of Kea while our research submarine prepares to dive to the wreck.*
Below: *A side-scan sonar "photograph" of the* Britannic *wreck.*
Right: *A bottom view of* NR-1 *taken from one of two ROVs.*

Left: *A pair of Welin davits, similar to those on the* Titanic *and* Olympic *(below), still fixed to the* Britannic*'s hull.*

Right: *The ship's whistle is still firmly attached to one of the funnels, which now lies on the ocean floor.*

touch the ship. In 3-D the propellers looked monstrous.

Because the wreck lies just two miles from shore, I expected it to resemble the nightmarish tangle of fishnets we'd encountered on the *Lusitania*. Instead, as we made our first pass over the hull, I began to realize we were in for something special. Not only was the ship in virtually one piece, but it was also almost completely free of these menaces. By the time *NR-1* resurfaced after a day underwater, I was elated. Our exploration over the next six days would fill in important details, but the big picture was already clear.

The *Britannic* lies on its starboard side at a list of about 85 degrees except for the tip of the bow, which sits slightly more upright, having almost wrenched free when it hit the bottom. From the well deck, a gaping tear extends down the visible port side of the hull and disappears into the bottom sediment. Along this tear some of the hull plating is bent upward, raising the question whether an internal explosion—possibly of coal dust from the forward reserve bunker—contributed to the sinking. But it seems most likely that the force of the impact is to blame. In fact, the tear occurs in roughly the same place where the *Titanic*'s bow buckled. The hull plating along the first sixty feet of the bow, which bore the brunt of the collision with the bottom, is horribly twisted and contorted. But the rest of the ship remains in remarkable condition, retaining its full ninety-four-foot width and much of the original superstructure, including deckhouses, cargo cranes, lifeboat davits, ventilators, capstans and railings. Were it not for the damage forward and the encrustations of marine life that blanket much of the wreck, the ship would look almost ready to rise up and continue

its voyage. And only at the almost perfectly preserved stern, with those massive propellers still in place, did we run into one of those treacherous fishnets. It was draped over the rudder.

Because the ship sank intact and lies so shallow, the yield from the tiny debris field was scanty—except for the four funnels (Cousteau spotted only one of these). Observers saw three of them fall off the sinking ship as it rolled over, and their positions on the seafloor reinforce this assertion. The longer the distance to the bottom, the more time there is for a ship to break apart, and the more time there is for the submarine current to distribute the debris. The number-one funnel lies only a few feet from its original position just aft of the bridge; presumably it fell off only on impact. The other three are spaced away from the ship, the farthest roughly five hundred feet away. Though flattened, they retain some of their elliptical shape and most of their original accoutrements, including ladders, steampipes and whistles. All in all, the funnels are in an amazing state of preservation.

Neither the main wreck nor the debris field shed any light on the continuing controversy over what sank the ship. Despite strong circumstantial evidence that a mine did the initial damage, some survivors swore they saw a torpedo track before the explosion. Perhaps we could find the mine anchor left behind when—and if—a mine exploded. An anchor would provide conclusive physical evidence of mines in the area. With only a few hours to spare from our investigation of the wreck, we followed the direction pointed by the debris trail—composed primarily of the three funnels that fell off as she sank—leading to the northwest of the wreck site. Presumably this was

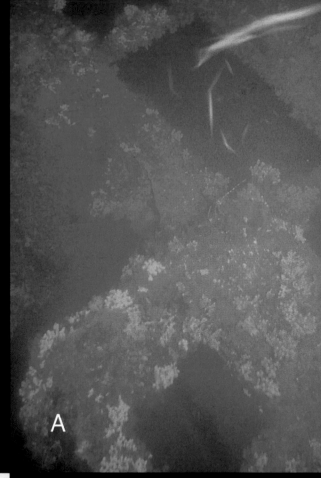

A

A. *A view of the small house on the port bridge wing, used by the captain to maneuver the ship in port or by lookouts at sea.*
B. *Another view of the port bridge wing.*
C. *The covered promenade deck.*

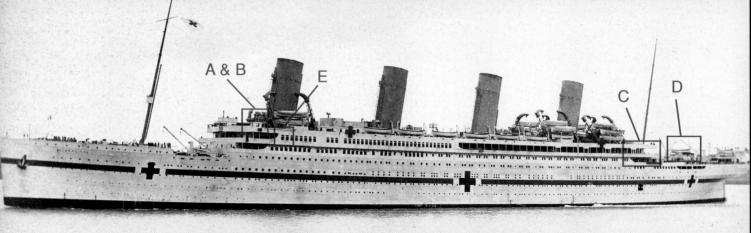

the path taken as Captain Bartlett briefly attempted to beach his ship. But our short search turned up no evidence of a mine anchor. The strong likelihood that a mine sank the ship cannot yet be called a certainty.

Nor can the visible evidence on the seafloor shed much light on why the ship sank as fast as she did, in only fifty-five minutes. I'm convinced that the tear in the hull at the well deck is the result of structural failure, not an internal explosion. We did see open portholes, certainly a contributing factor, but could these alone explain the swift demise of a ship expressly designed to survive such limited damage? Perhaps someday, if we return to send a robot vehicle inside the bow, we will learn more.

B

C

D

E

D. *The ship's aft docking bridge, used to maneuver the ship to and away from pier side.*
E. *The forward end of the ship's enclosed promenade deck.*
Britannic *was to have been the greatest of all White Star liners; sadly, no peacetime passenger ever walked these decks.*

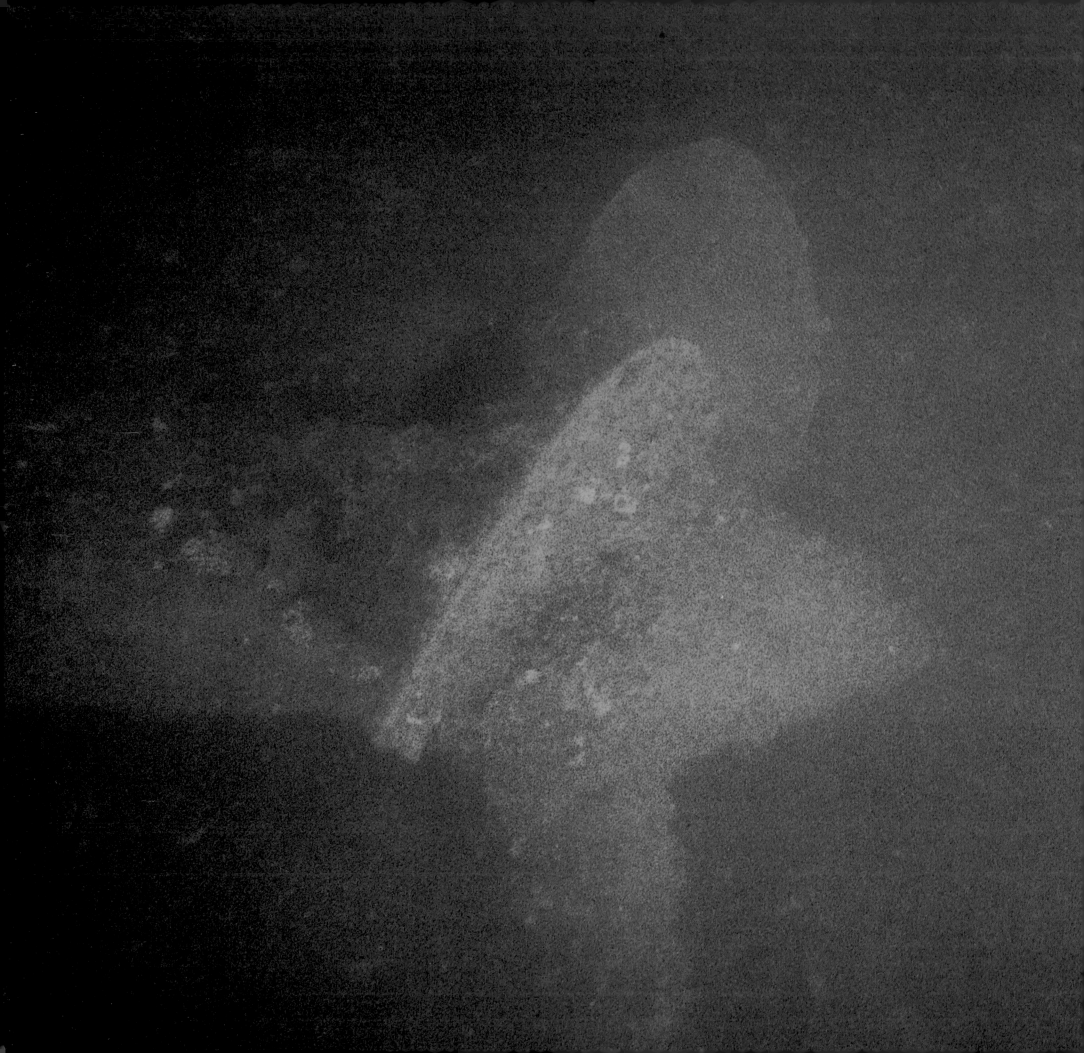

Opposite: *The port propeller is completely visible. Beneath the ship, the starboard prop is also visible.*
Below: *The port and center propellers from* Britannic*'s sister* Olympic.
Bottom and right: *A model of one of the ship's huge gantry davits and the top of one of these lifeboat-launching cranes as it looks today.*

Chapter

5

The First World War set back
the progress of the transatlantic liner,
but not for long. By the late twenties,
marvelous new ships of startling
interior design and even more startling
speed attracted a whole new type of
passenger, the middle-class tourist.
But with the appearance of the French
Line's *Normandie* in 1935 and
Cunard's *Queen Mary* in 1936,
the passenger realized a romantic ideal
of style that now seems out of reach.

The new Normandie **passes the venerable old Cunarder**
Aquitania **in mid-Atlantic, summer 1935.**

High-Seas Society

Normandie, Queen Mary *and the Rise of Glamour,*
1919 ~ 1945

World War I had cut short a golden age of transatlantic travel just as it was approaching its climax. In the war's wake, the great steamship lines faced a more uncertain world and faced it with fewer resources. White Star's *Britannic* and Cunard's *Lusitania* lay on the sea bottom. But worst off was Hamburg-Amerika, whose three greatest liners went to the Allies as part of the punishing war reparations called for in the Treaty of Versailles. The *Vaterland* became the USS *Leviathan*. *Imperator* became *Berengaria*, joining the *Mauretania* and the *Aquitania* on Cunard's Southampton-New York run. And the *Bismarck*, which had lain unfinished in Hamburg's Blohm and Voss shipyards throughout the war, became White Star's brand-new *Majestic*, a worthy companion for the bereaved *Olympic*.

Refitted to their prewar splendor and converted from coal to oil, these great ships resumed their routes, but traveled them far less than full. In Britain and America the wealthy, leisured classes enjoyed less wealth and leisure, while the flood tide of European emigration suddenly ebbed as the United States withdrew into isolationism. The Dillingham Immigration Act of 1921 reduced the annual flow from a million

Above: *In the aftermath of World War I, the Germans lost their three greatest liners. The* Imperator *became Cunard's* Berengaria, *the Bismarck was reincarnated as White Star's* Majestic, *and the* Vaterland *joined the United States Lines as* Leviathan.

Opposite: *Sailing first class on board these reborn superliners, one encountered 1920s style combined with prewar luxe. The Berengaria's dining saloon (bottom left) retained its late Edwardian splendor, but on the Leviathan the prewar Palm Court became a Jazz Age nightclub (bottom right).*

immigrants a year to barely a trickle. Clearly this was not a time for building bigger ships or investing in technology designed to shatter existing speed records. The real question was whether passenger traffic would ever rebound to its prewar levels.

The salvation of the transatlantic service turned out to be the rise of the modern tourist—not the wealthy cosmopolite undertaking a lengthy grand tour but the middle-class American of moderate means and the student with a summer to kill. Faced with vast amounts of unbooked space, especially in third class, creative travel agents

persuaded the steamship companies to repackage their more Spartan accommodations as "tourist third cabin." As the idea caught on, many ships were refitted to improve their tourist quarters, replacing all accommodation below first class with various gradations within tourist class. But it was not until after World War II and the rise of the cruise ship that whole vessels were built without class divisions. On these modern vessels, a wealthy passenger can still book an expensive suite, but everyone eats in the same dining room and has access to all the same facilities.

First class remained a fixture on most liners through the booming twenties, but the makeup of its clientele began to change. More and more these well-heeled travelers belonged to the nouveau riche eager to act out their social fantasies for the duration of a voyage. All one needed was a copy of *Emily Post* and a set of evening clothes. Meanwhile a luminous new elite began replacing the fading lights of the European aristocracy and old money, the motion-picture stars and movie moguls who increasingly became the real celebrities of the postwar world.

As passenger numbers gradually recovered, new ships appeared, but none to rival the prewar grandiosities still plying their stately trade. In fact, the first new liner of

Left: An advertisement for the Leviathan emphasizes the change from prewar days. Now the great ships depended on middle-class tourists looking for an affordable holiday instead of poor immigrants hoping for a fresh start in America.

Opposite above: The first major new passenger ship on the Atlantic scene was the French Line's Ile de France, famed for both its decor and its first-class service.

Opposite below: The view along the Ile de France's promenade deck.

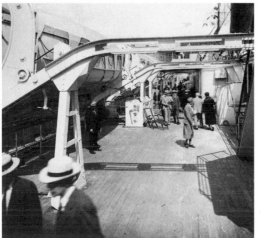

note is remembered not for her size or her technological originality but for her interior decoration. She was the *Ile de France* of 1927, the latest creation of the Compagnie Générale Transatlantique (CGT), commonly known as the French Line. CGT, a relative latecomer to the speed and luxury sweepstakes, had only commissioned its first serious contender, the *France*, in 1912, which embarked on her maiden voyage only five days after the *Titanic* sank. That ship, barely half the size of the *Titanic*, made its mark as the "Chateau of the Atlantic," with interiors modeled after the splendid excess of Louis XIV's palace at Versailles. "I doubt that any craft since Cleopatra's fabled barge knew such visual extravagance," comments John Maxtone-Graham.

By contrast, the interiors of the *Ile de France* represented something new. For the first time, a ship's passenger spaces had been designed not to reproduce decorative styles of the past but to celebrate a style of the present. Her fitting-out followed the famous Paris Exposition des Arts Decoratifs et Industriels Modernes of 1925, which gave the world the term art deco and inspired the *Ile*'s contemporary style. The result, depending on your perspective, was either sublime or over the top—her interiors included a complete imitation of a Parisian sidewalk café—but passengers took to her immediately, especially Americans hungry for a soupçon of French sophistication. She

Above: *Often referred to as "the Chateau of the Atlantic," the prewar liner France of 1912 evinced traditional Gallic flair — right down to a picture of Louis XIV over the fireplace in her first-class lounge.*

Above: *By contrast, the first-class entrance hall of the* Ile de France *represented a striking departure from liner tradition, a ship decorated in a contemporary style, in this case the brand-new art deco.*

quickly became the chosen ship of "the youthful, the stylish and the famous," to quote John Malcolm Brinnin, favored by the likes of John D. Rockefeller, Arturo Toscanini and Tallulah Bankhead. But they did not choose her for her speed. She was roughly as fast as the *Aquitania* of 1914—and no larger.

Remarkably, the year the *Ile de France* entered service, the venerable *Mauretania* still held the Blue Riband. More remarkable still, the country to win it from her would be Germany. Somehow, out of the ruins of war, North German Lloyd, creator of the *Kaiser Wilhelm der Grosse*, the first German ship to snatch the speed record from the

British just before the turn of the century, managed to rebuild its fortunes and raise enough capital to contemplate the building of two record-breaking ships, *Bremen* and *Europa*.

The two ships would be about the size of the prewar German giants, but there the similarity would end. The first big difference was their shape. Viewed bow on, the ships had hulls that bulged outward, and the lower bow ended in a strange bulbous protuberance. Their squat funnels and streamlined superstructures gave them a look of almost menacing modernity. And, although sharply at odds with the kitschiness of many of the decorative touches, their starkly functional interiors had an almost clinical severity. These ships meant business.

On *Bremen*'s maiden voyage in July of 1929, she sliced eight hours off the *Mauretania*'s best time, while averaging an unheard-of 27.9 knots. (In August the *Mauretania* made one last valiant effort, beating her own best time by five hours, but she couldn't catch the new ocean greyhound.) On *Europa*'s maiden voyage a year later—she had been delayed by a fire that had

Right: *The* Bremen *and her sister,* Europa, *pass at sea.*

destroyed her nearly complete interiors—she narrowly beat the *Bremen*. Soon these two fast, modern ships had captured the lion's share of the transatlantic passenger trade, forcing some sort of response from the rival lines. At last it seemed that something akin to the great prewar rivalry for speed might be revived.

Out of this competitive climate emerged plans for three great ships a thousand feet in length and able to maintain an average speed of 30 knots: White Star's *Oceanic*, Cunard's *Queen Mary* and CGT's *Normandie*. When these ships were paired with an equally fast sister, each company would finally achieve the long-held dream of a two-ship weekly service between New York and Europe. In the heady days of the late 1920s, such an eventuality seemed a certainty.

Plans for all three ships were well advanced before the stock-market crash of October 1929, but only the *Oceanic* was already under way in the Harland & Wolff shipyards of Belfast, which had built the *Titanic* and her two fabulous siblings. Not

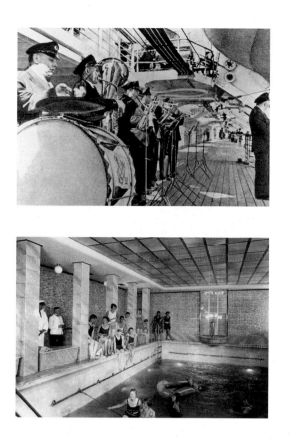

Bremen *and* Europa *quickly became the North Atlantic's most popular ships, boasting not only all the amenities that the late 1920s could offer, including a splendid pool in the International Style (above) and a special catapult-launched aircraft to speed the arrival of the mail (opposite below). Only Germany's airships (below) offered a faster way to cross.*

until December of 1930 did work begin on the *Queen Mary* in the Clydebank yards of John Brown and Co., where the *Lusitania* had first seen the light. Cunard's directors saw the deepening depression as a chance to build their new ship cheaply in anticipation of the economic recovery soon to come. A few weeks later, in January 1931, work finally began on the *Normandie* at the French Line's own yards at St. Nazaire, where the *Ile de France* and her forebears had been born. France had so far been unaffected by the economic downturn.

But the aura of steamship optimism had already begun to dissipate. White Star, whose financial position had always been the most tenuous, canceled construction of the partly built *Oceanic* soon after the Crash. Cunard, faced with sharply falling revenue, put all work on hold in December 1931, but kept on a skeleton staff to maintain the ship against an eventual restart of construction. Only the *Normandie* continued to grow apace, thanks to generous subsidies from the French government, support that became increasingly controversial as the economic situation deteriorated.

On October 29, 1932, three years to the day after the Great Crash, two hundred thousand people watched the *Normandie* slip into the Loire River at St. Nazaire under threatening skies. Mme Albert Lebrun, wife of the French president, performed the champagne ritual. "The largest moving object mankind had ever created," to quote the ship's biographer Harvey Ardman, caused a huge backwash that nearly drowned several spectators. But the revolutionary hull design of the first ship ever to exceed a thousand feet in length made a more lasting impression than her great size. Nothing quite like her had ever been seen before.

Above the waterline, she cut a rakish figure with her forward-thrusting, clipperlike bow. Her lower hull looked awkward and ungainly—hardly built for speed. She had a bulbous forefoot reminiscent of *Bremen* and *Europa* and a pear-shaped middle that "appeared to sag ponderously like the thighs of a supine fat lady," to quote John Maxtone-Graham. Yet this combination produced a hull of unprecedented hydrodynamic efficiency, yielding almost no bow wave and leaving a thin flat wake. During her initial speed trials, skeptical French fishermen were so impressed that they commented, "She skims over the water like a seagull." Even when the *Normandie* passed at high speed, a small boat had little to fear from her satellite waves.

Ironically for a ship that was the product of French national pride and that soon came to epitomize Gallic flair, the concept for the *Normandie*'s hull originated from a Russian émigré named Vladimir Yourkevitch, then toiling on the assembly line of the Renault factory in Paris. Before the Russian Revolution, Yourkevitch had designed warships for the Russian navy, credentials good enough to convince the directors of CGT to give his proposals a try. To their astonishment, the models made to his specifications consistently outperformed more traditional hull shapes in the test tanks, finally convincing the French to adopt his radical configuration. (Yourkevitch later tried to market his concept to the British, but they were less willing than the French to consider alien expertise.)

The superstructure that gradually rose from this prototypical hull was equally radical, cleanly swept and aerodynamically streamlined like none before. A giant teak-colored whaleback concealed the foredeck and its clutter of ropes and chains, winches and capstans, ending halfway to the bridge with an elegant breakwater. The bridge and its wings met the onrushing air in a graceful curve. The three funnels, each one slightly shorter than the one before, were teardrop-shaped in cross section, another touch of aerodynamic sophistication. Between the funnels stretched virtually uncluttered expanses of teak decking available for passenger recreation. And the afterdecks stepped down in a delightful cascade to the stern. It seemed that everything that could be done had been done to make *Normandie* a ship without peer.

Because of the continuing slump in passenger traffic, her debut, originally scheduled for 1934, was delayed until late May 1935. In the meantime, an artful publicity

Below: Normandie's *stylish prow gave no hint of the bulbous protuberance below the waterline designed to reduce water resistance.*
Bottom: *At her stern, the* Normandie's *superstructure descended to the hull in a series of graceful steps.*

It is May 29, 1935, and the Normandie prepares to set sail from the French Line's modernistic new terminal at Le Havre.

machine had captured massive public interest, especially in the United States, the potential source of many of her future passengers. In inimitable fashion, the French turned *Normandie*'s impending maiden voyage into the occasion for a series of presailing galas that must have left her kitchen staff and stewards sighing with relief when the ship finally left port. For three days in succession, the *Normandie* hosted luxurious banquets and provided sumptuous entertainments for thousands of guests, many of whom later slept in cabins and staterooms that had lacked beds or washbasins only hours before their arrival.

Nothing, however, could overshadow the glamour of the *Normandie*'s maiden voyage or diminish the elevated expectations attending it. The advance publicity, the press coverage and now the reports brought back by the guests at her prevoyage galas confirmed that she was a ship of breathtaking beauty and grandeur. She was also reputed to be a vessel of unprecedented speed. During her trials in early May, she had easily reached a speed of 32 knots, holding out the promise that her maiden voyage would also be a record-breaking one.

Few passengers were thinking about speed as the tugs drew the *Normandie* away from her home pier in Le Havre just after 5:00 p.m. on May 29, 1935. They were more interested in exploring the amazing new ship as it sped across the Channel to Southampton. What they discovered, at least those fortunate enough to travel first class, was a grandeur of conception and an attention to detail unparalleled before or since. Two duos of architects had designed her interior spaces, and a team of renowned French artists and designers were responsible for the ship's interior decor.

What must have impressed those inaugural voyagers most of all was the profligate sense of space. Most older liners had given over a great deal of their interiors to the uptakes that carried smoke from the engine rooms up to the ship's funnels. The *Normandie*'s designers split the uptakes of the two working funnels and ran them up the outside of the superstructure. This strategy, first tried by the *Vaterland* in 1914 but never imitated by the British, gave the new ship sweeping interior spaces. The grand salon, which rose to a vaulted peak three decks high, was only one of a series of inter-connected rooms and avenues on the promenade deck that could form an uninter-rupted concourse of unprecedented length when the sliding wooden panels between the grand salon and the almost equally impressive smoking room were open. A French journalist on the maiden voyage described the *Normandie* as "the grand hotel of one's dreams, as only a Hollywood producer might conceive it." Certainly it was easy to forget one was on board a ship at all. "But where is the boat? . . . I want to see the boat!" a small boy would later exclaim on encountering her seemingly endless public spaces.

In such overweening surroundings, it must have been easy to feel that one was in fact playing a role in a Hollywood musical or some other grand theatrical event. On a subsequent voyage, the noted British writer and diplomat Harold Nicolson observed that "the whole place is like the setting for a ballet. Choruses of stewards, sailors, fire-men, stewardesses, engineers, and passengers. There are also some fifty liftiers in bright

Top: Upon emerging from the café grill, one's view swept down a grand staircase to the magnificent smoking room. Above: A stylized view of the smoking room showing the grand staircase. Opposite: Beyond the smoking room lay the even more impressive grand salon, which in the evening often became a glamorous night-club.

Normandie's first-class, or cabin-class, dining room was located two decks below the spectacular promenade deck's grande allée. This Hollywood-scale temple of haute cuisine, dressed in a dazzling array of gold and white and bathed in a shimmering shower of light, was in its day the largest room afloat, able to accommodate all of first class in a single seating.

scarlet who look like the petals of salvias flying about these golden corridors. That is the essential effect—gold, Lalique glass and scarlet."

The climactic act of the daily shipboard spectacle was dinner, convened at the exotic hour to American passengers of 8:00 p.m. The ships of the French Line had always been known for their fine food—and the *Normandie*'s cuisine was as fine as any that has ever been served on board ship—but no previous vessel had constructed a kind of culinary cathedral for its consumption. The *Normandie*'s dining room was quite simply the largest room afloat before or since, 305 feet long and 45 feet wide, with a coffered ceiling 26 feet high; it provided space for 150 tables with places for seven hundred diners. Overlooking the scene stood *La Paix*, a tall slender statue of a woman wearing a toga, one hand raised to offer an olive branch. Elaborate bas-reliefs graced the walls at either end.

Despite the publicists' comparisons to the Hall of Mirrors at Versailles (this room was slightly longer), the *Normandie*'s dining room was above all a hall of light. Its simple, long rectangular nave was lit by twelve tall stalagmites of Lalique glass and thirty-eight towering columns of light that lined the walls. Within such a feast of luminosity the two chandeliers that hung at each end of the coffered ceiling seemed almost an afterthought. All that was lacking to make the movie metaphor complete was a spotlight trained on the *grande descente*, the staircase down which every diner made a ritual entrance before the eyes of all.

On the maiden voyage, with the first-class ladies wearing the latest fashions of famous Paris designers such as Chanel, Worth and Patou, the display must have been a dazzling one. Some women even took advantage of the room's air conditioning—another *Normandie* first— to wrap their shoulders in expensive furs. In addition to the ship's "godmother," Mme LeBrun, the glittering passenger list included two counts and countesses, a bevy of wealthy Americans and several luminaries of stage, screen, literature and politics. The Comte and Comtesse de Tocqueville had a special reason for making the trip: among the several handsome gifts from France being carried to America was a bust of the count's illustrious ancestor, Alexis, to be presented to President Franklin Roosevelt. One of the most famous travelers was the French novelist Colette, who found the scale of the dining room overwhelming. In her notebook she described ordering for breakfast "what, by contrast, strikes me as the tiniest *café au lait* in the world."

Over the course of the *Normandie*'s short life, the dining room would be the setting for its share of high-society dramas. In October 1935, for example, Josephine Baker, the African-American star of Paris's Folies Bergères, was returning to America to appear in a new rendition of *The Ziegfeld Follies*. For the first few evenings, seasickness kept her in her deluxe suite, but she roused herself when she discovered there was another star on board, the almost equally famous Billie Burke, who happened to be Ziegfeld's widow. Miss Baker sent Miss Burke an invitation to join her for dinner, which, apparently, was accepted. When Baker appeared at the top of the staircase, sheathed in a sheer, pale yellow gown by Erté, the entire dining room gave her a standing ovation. But Billie Burke upstaged her, making her own grand entrance, then approaching Baker's table only to flash her a look of withering scorn, before passing on without saying a word. Miss Baker ate her meal alone, proceeded to the top of the stair, turned and rewarded the assembly with a radiant smile, which earned her yet another round of applause and surely the last word of the evening, which reportedly was, "I assume she belongs to the black-hating race."

After dinner many of the guests proceeded to the theater, the first ever on shipboard, which doubled as both live stage and cinema. One evening the theater held a benefit hosted by Colette and the famous French actress Marcelle Chantal. Later a variety show might be presented in the grand lounge. And, until the wee hours of the morning, there was dancing in the café grill to the strains of either the French Tango Orchestra or Crisler's Jazz Orchestra.

Once the café grill finally opened on June 1—artisans had worked frantically to finish it as the maiden voyage got under way—the grill became one of the most popular spots on the *Normandie*, tripling as bar, à la carte restaurant and nightclub. Perched at the aft end of the superstructure, reached by a stately staircase with five landings and topped by another tall, elegant statue, it was the culmination of the promenade deck's *grande allée*, the uninterupted concourse that led from the theater through the grand salon and the smoking room.

Top: *Normandie's theater, the first ever on board a ship, was designed for both movies and live theatricals.*
Above: *A theater program.*

The Normandie's café grill departed from the prevailing design mode of the ship to follow a more starkly modern style. The grill occupied the farthest aft part of the promenade deck, the last in a line of remarkable public rooms that ran from the theater through the grand hall and grand salon to the smoking room.

In contrast to the lavish, late-art-deco style of most of the ship's public rooms, the café grill, with its stainless-steel-frame, black-leather chairs, square black columns and engraved-glass bar, provided a true taste of the modern functionalism championed by France's Le Corbusier and the Bauhaus architects of Germany. Wide picture windows gave diners and dancers a panoramic ocean view, making the room one of the few places on board where one had a true sense of being on a ship at sea. In the foreground was the first of the decks stepping down toward the stern, home to the terrace bar, an open air veranda protected from the wind by the superstructure and by windbreaks formed of high-backed benches arranged in an elegant zigzag pattern.

First-class revels undoubtedly continued late into the night in many of the *Normandie*'s splendid staterooms and deluxe suites, though likely not in the two most

Nothing as stylish as the Normandie's first-class suites and staterooms had ever been seen at sea before.
Left: *The Deauville Suite, one of two* apartements de grand luxe *on the sun deck.*
Above and right: *Only slightly less fabulous were the* apartements de luxe *and of these the Rouen Suite, which featured walls covered in lacquer and pigskin, was among the most magnificent.*

deluxe apartments of all, situated at the aft end of the sun deck, one deck above the café grill. On the maiden voyage, the starboard side Trouville Suite was occupied by Mme Lebrun and her entourage. The port side Deauville Suite was the preserve of the Maharajah of Kapurtala, whose Hindu cook prepared a special Indian dinner one evening for Madame Lebrun and Admiral Maurice Bigot, her naval attaché.

Each the work of an individual designer, these unique apartments included four bedrooms, a sitting room, a dining room with serving pantry and a private terrace. They were furnished with specially designed furniture and decorated with choice objets d'art and original Aubusson tapestries.

But these were only the most airy and opulent of the *Normandie*'s first-class accommodations. Two more deluxe suites on the main deck, along with ten *apartements de luxe*, likewise the work of individual artists, were almost as lavish and in some cases even more visually stunning. Nor were the more ordinary staterooms anything to complain about. The more than four hundred first-class staterooms, three-quarters with portholes opening onto the sea, were the work of thirty interior designers who created forty distinct designs. Even then, no two cabins were identical and no two cabins of like design sat next to each other.

More than any superliner before or since, the *Normandie* was a first-class ship. Seventy-five percent of her passenger space (public rooms and private sleeping quarters) was devoted to her wealthiest customers and almost half of her 1,972 berths — 864—were dedicated to those who could afford to travel in style. (Tourist class slept 654 and third class 454.) Her ratio of staff to passengers was the highest ever. What's more, the largest ship to date carried far fewer total passengers than had the smaller "luxury" liners built before the war, yielding the greatest amenity of all for the ocean traveler, the luxury of ample private space. True, the smallest (and cheapest) first-class cabin was an eight-foot-by-eight-foot cubicle (presumably favored by travelers who did more dancing than sleeping), but most of the first-class rooms on the *Normandie* had space to spare. And her public areas were the grandest ever. One detail, however, highlights the different expectations of comfort and convenience now and then. Thirty first-class cabins had shared bathrooms.

At breakfast, which was typically sparsely attended, the dining room must have seemed cavernous and somewhat alienating, but early risers not nursing a hangover had the run of the ship and a feast of possibilities to help them pass the day. If it was Sunday, there would be services in the magnificent chapel, yet another *Normandie* first (a synagogue was added in 1936). One's after-breakfast stroll might lead one to the winter garden at the forwardmost point of the promenade deck, which provided a broad view over the bow amid lush greenery, burbling fountains and the trilling of exotic birds. The library held five thousand volumes and the high-modern swimming pool was not only the largest ever on shipboard, but was sloped from the shallow end, with the increasing depths marked off with black rubber posts. There was also a shooting gallery and a gymnasium. Boxing and fencing lessons could be had by appointment. A rather windy tennis court was found on the sports deck, located between the first and second funnels. Just aft of that was the dog-walking track, where dog owners could take their pets from the kennel housed inside the dummy third funnel. You could shop at a special outlet of Paris' swank Bon Marché department store, make an appointment at the hair salon or barber shop or order flowers for your paramour at the flower shop. If you were particularly privileged—that is, rich or famous enough—you might be invited to dine with the captain.

Above: *Passengers playing deck tennis — a ring tossed back and forth — on the Normandie's topmost deck.*
Opposite: *Captain René Pugnet's private suite was dominated by a picture of the captain himself.*

Captain René Pugnet's private suite on the sun deck just aft of the bridge rivaled the most luxurious first-class apartments. With its dining/reception room measuring thirty-one feet by eighteen (the ceiling was nine feet high) and its private terrace, it was clearly designed for entertaining. If you were lucky, Pugnet might treat you to a postprandial serenade on violin or piano—he was an accomplished musician who liked to build his own instruments. Whether your native tongue was French, German,

Spanish or English, he would address you in your own language. An amateur aviator, a pioneer of color photography, a decent portrait painter, the *Normandie*'s commander was a man of unusual refinement—not to mention a very fine seaman whose career had begun in the days of sail—undoubtedly the perfect captain for such a stylish ship.

Besides the captain, the man who most set the tone in first class and did most to assure that the new ship would become the choice of high society was Purser Henri Villar, a former lawyer who had made his reputation on the fashionable *Ile de France*. So charming, witty and urbane was Villar that the oceangoing elite were accustomed to fitting their travel schedules to his sailing dates. It was he who ran the floating grand hotel that was the *Normandie* with unfailing diplomacy. If you had sailed with him before, he would greet you by name as you came on board and make you feel as if you were his personal guest.

We can be sure that Villar handled more than a few complaints on this maiden voyage, since the ship had sailed before it was quite finished. Only hours before departure had plumbers completed installing the washbasins for many first-class staterooms, and work continued elsewhere throughout the maiden voyage. (Most of the passengers in third class were workmen.) But the ship was so wonderful and her progress so impressive that most complaints soon evaporated into the salt air. Most, but not all.

Sitting in the café grill, passengers experienced an unsettling vibration. Harold Nicolson noted that "the flowers on the little tables wobble something dreadful and it would be difficult to read for long." Throughout most of first class, the vibration was scarcely noticeable, but tourist class and the crew's quarters lower down in the stern suffered so severely that a number of passengers were moved to different cabins farther forward. (The problem had been noted during the ship's initial trials and addressed, inadequately it turned out, by some last-minute strengthening in the stern.) It was a problem that had haunted express liners throughout the age of steam. But would the solution, as with the *Mauretania*, prove to be reengineering the propellers, or was it a problem more fundamental, some previously undetected flaw in Yourkevitch's hull?

Such worries did little to dampen the general enthusiasm, particularly as with each passing day the likelihood increased that this would be a record-breaking voyage. By the morning of June 2, Captain Pugnet was so confident that he told the press, "We

Purser Henri Villar's legendary skill at making first-class passengers feel special made him second only to the captain in the ship's hierarchy.

The Normandie *approaches her New York pier for the first time.*

shan't try very hard on this trip, but we shall break all records easily." Just past 11:00 a.m. the following day, *Normandie* came abreast of the Ambrose Lightship, the official finishing line of the nearly three-thousand-mile westward dash across the Atlantic. She had covered the distance in four days, three hours and two minutes, averaging fractionally under 30 knots for the entire crossing.

The *Normandie*'s maiden voyage established her as the class of the North Atlantic, *the* ship to travel on. And if there were any doubts about her speed, she captured the eastbound Blue Riband on her return trip. All signs seemed to herald a long and profitable career. Certainly the rich, the fashionable and the celebrated, the cream of high-seas society, flocked to travel on her. And her passenger lists over the next four years read like a *Who's Who* of business, arts and entertainment. On one wonderful occasion, both Cole Porter and Noel Coward were on board. Perhaps they got together in the grand salon after dinner to accompany each other on the grand piano. Movie stars seemed to love her, and she seldom made a voyage without a few of Hollywood's leading lights: Edward G. Robinson, Gloria Swanson, Douglas Fairbanks Jr., Fred Astaire, Leslie Howard, Olivia de Havilland, George Raft, Marlene Dietrich—the list seems endless. A passage on the *Normandie* came to be equated with glamour.

The problem with vibration was soon solved by new propellers, but not before the first-class terrace aft of the café grill had been replaced with a tourist-class lounge that added stiffening but stole much of the magnificent view and made the Trouville and Deauville suites a little less desirable. The first time Marlene Dietrich emerged onto her "private" terrace, she found herself gawked at by a crowd of tourist-class passengers playing games on the new lounge's roof deck. All in all, however, the *Normandie* lived up to every expectation. She lacked only a worthy rival.

In April 1934, after nearly two and a half years lying rusting in the John Brown shipyards, work had finally recommenced on the future *Queen Mary*. Following a merger between Cunard and the fast-falling White Star Line, which was effectively swallowed by her old rival, the British government loaned the newly formed Cunard White Star Line enough money to finish the ship. More powerful than any economic argument, the imminent launch of the *Normandie* threatened Britain's maritime pride and helped ensure government intervention. Workmen at the John Brown shipyards spent the first few weeks evicting several thousand rooks that had nested in the scaffolding and crane gantries and removing tons of accumulated rust. But the hull remained sound.

Queen Mary, wife of George V, christened and launched her the following September. (The name was a deliberate compromise designed to avoid Cunard's tradition of ending ships in *ia* and White Star's standard *ic* ending.) By early in 1936, her fitting-out was complete. At the end of March when she steamed into Southampton Water for the first time, it was clear to any observer that apart from her size she was a throwback to an earlier era, a stately, old-fashioned-looking descendant of the *Mauretania* by way of the *Aquitania*.

The Queen Mary during fitting out at the John Brown shipyards in Glasgow.

The *Queen Mary* was almost as long as the *Normandie* and occupied almost as many gross tons of hull volume, but besides the closeness in size, the two ships could not have been more different. Where the *Normandie* seemed daring and stylish and slightly risqué, the *Queen Mary* emanated an aura of solid, stolid reliability. Her profile was graceful, if traditional. Her hand-picked staff and crew impeccably maintained the unmatched Cunard tradition of personal service. Her interior spaces were almost as vast and impressive as those of her French rival. But she managed, especially in the decoration of her staterooms, to seem a little dowdy almost from the day she was born.

Ocean liner historians have tended to dismiss the interiors of the *Queen Mary* as a mediocre mélange of the conventional and the modern, in contrast to what might almost be called the artsy snobbery of the *Normandie*. John Malcolm Brinnin goes so far as to suggest that she had the "atmosphere of an enormous sanitarium." If her designers and decorators had rejected the grab-bag historicism of an earlier era, he and others argue, they had failed to find a contemporary style worthy of the largest British ship yet built. It was not that the *Queen Mary* had been decorated on the cheap. Her interiors boasted more than fifty different woods, inspiring one admirer to write that "the forests of the British Empire have been searched for these rare and magnificent veneers." But her critics have preferred to dwell upon what they see as the overuse of newly developed synthetics, such as rayon, linoleum and Formica, this last covering the tops of furniture and lining the bathroom walls in even the most luxurious first-class suites. The floor of the dining room, in its own way as impressive as the *Normandie*'s, was made of something called Korkoid, giving the effect, according to Brinnin, of "a duchess in flowing chiffon and sparkling tiara who, close up, is seen to be wearing jogging shoes." (Brinnin neglects to mention that the *Normandie*'s dining-room floor was made of exactly the same material.) To the *Queen Mary*'s detractors, the overall decorative scheme yielded cacaphony not harmony, cheapness rather than luxe, vulgarity rather than refinement. One contemporary commentator summed up this majority opinion as follows: "The workmanship is magnificent, the materials used are splendid, the result is appalling."

Yet had the *Queen Mary* entered service at any time other than the year after her

Above: *An embarkation pamphlet shows the* Queen Mary *under full steam.*
Opposite: *Not as breathtakingly beautiful as the* Normandie, *the* Queen Mary *was still a spectacularly modern ship. Her first-class lounge (near right), her forward observation lounge (top right), her palatial dining saloon (middle right) and her indoor pool (bottom right) all indicate just how striking her interiors could be.*

Opposite and below: The Queen Mary *wasn't afraid to look like a ship. Her staterooms displayed nautical touches and her decks had a traditional look.*
Bottom: The Queen Mary *takes on passengers at Cherbourg.*
Overleaf: The Queen Mary *under full steam en route to New York.*

great French rival, she would undoubtedly have come down to us as the most beautiful and comfortable ship of her era. Her public rooms were splendid, decorated with fine paintings and sculptures from contemporary British artists. The new synthetics that now seem a trifle tacky were then extremely expensive, the acme of 1930s luxury. *The Shipbuilder*, being a British publication, undoubtedly overstates the case but helps restore some balance: "The modern influence undoubtedly exists, but rampant modernity has been studiously and successfully avoided. The result is everywhere delightful, the beautifully balanced decorations and appointments combining to produce an atmosphere of rich, although unobtrusive, luxury which pervades the whole vessel."

The *Normandie's* grandiosity gained her lasting fame, but it did not make her popular. She seldom traveled full, while passengers flocked to the *Queen Mary* throughout her long career, preferring the British ship's unpretentiousness and her somewhat more homey comforts to the *Normandie's* movie-star glitter and overwhelming scale. Despite her great size, the *Queen Mary* was still proud to be a ship, with her brass-rimmed portholes, her solid wooden deck chairs and her familiar Cunard profile. Not surprisingly, the British aristocracy favored her, but so did businessmen and tourists by the thousands. Somehow she transcended her flaws. The legions who traveled on her year after year—many of them again and again—loved her in spite of them and ensured that she would become a legend.

At the beginning, the *Queen Mary's* flaws included the familiar problem of excessive vibration — largely corrected through interior stiffening and propeller redesign — smokestacks that littered the afterdeck with grimy grit, requiring the installation of expensive smoke-washing devices and, worst of all, an agonizing long slow roll in heavy seas. The *Normandie*, a so-called snappy roller who righted herself with almost disconcerting dispatch, seldom broke a plate in her first-class kitchen. However, the first time the *Queen Mary* encountered a real storm, in October of 1936, she gave her passengers and crew quite a scare. "She suddenly started to go and she went, so slowly, down and down and down," recalled one of her stewardesses. "I was thrown out of my bunk and thought that she was never coming back. . . . Slowly she righted herself and then began a horrible corkscrew motion that went on and on, even after the sea had become calm. She just didn't seem to be able to stop it."

No one had thought to install handrails in the passageways or to anchor any of her furniture—such a huge ship seemed to guarantee stability. Some passengers were injured; a few became hysterical. The damage to property was considerable. Replacing crockery and adding handrails didn't address the underlying problem, which wasn't solved until the late 1950s by the addition of stabilizer fins. But passengers grew used to the great ship's foibles and continued to flock to her. Her long, slow roll became part of the character that made her, in the words of her last commander, Captain J. Treasure-Jones, "the nearest ship ever to a living being."

Undeniably, a most winsome aspect of her personality was speed. If she failed to break the *Normandie*'s mark on her maiden voyage, the record was not long in coming. On August 31, 1936, she made the eastbound passage in three days, twenty-three hours and fifty-seven minutes, the first ship ever to manage the distance in under four days. Although the *Normandie* briefly regained the record in 1937, the *Queen Mary* soon won it back for good the following year. She was undeniably the faster ship. The *Normandie* had the more modern hull, but the *Queen Mary*'s engines could develop considerably more horsepower, which overcame her less efficient hull design. After 1938 her hold on the Blue Riband was unbroken until the summer of 1952, when the fastest superliner of them all, the *United States*, made its maiden voyage.

Both the *Normandie* and the *Queen Mary* had their promising careers interrupted by the outbreak of World War II; they spent its opening months moored in close proximity at their respective New York piers. In March 1940 they were joined by the not-quite-finished *Queen Elizabeth*, whose top-secret maiden voyage had been accomplished so that she could complete her fitting-out in the calm and safety of a neutral port. For two weeks, the world's three greatest ships lay side by side. Then the *Queen Mary* sailed for Australia, where her conversion to troopship would take place. Six months later, the *Elizabeth*, too, was gone.

For a time after the fall of France in May 1940, the *Normandie* languished in limbo. Maintained by a skeleton crew, "she seemed like a summer resort hotel that has been closed down for the winter," said the *New York Times*. After the ship was claimed by France's collaborationist Vichy government, the U.S. Coast Guard placed her in protective custody. Following Pearl Harbor, however, the U.S. Navy stepped in. There

was some argument over whether the famous passenger liner was better suited to conversion to an aircraft carrier or a troopship, but her unarmored hull settled the question. She would be refitted to rival the already successful Cunarders, whose wartime service soon became legendary.

On December 24, 1941, the *Normandie*'s fabulous fittings having been removed to New York warehouses, the massive conversion process began. Navy and civilian workers swarmed over the ship in round-the-clock shifts in a situation often bordering on chaos. A New York journalist wanting to test security easily passed himself off as a worker and proved how simple it would be to sabotage the ship. But the greatest hazard was the general disorganization, bred of impossible deadlines, bureaucratic ineptitude and a split command. To an impartial observer, the *Normandie*'s transformation into the troopship *Lafayette* was an accident waiting to happen.

Above: *The* Queen Elizabeth *approaches the Cunard pier in New York.*
Opposite: *For two weeks in March 1940, the two* Queens *and the* Normandie *lay side by side in New York harbor.*

In the early afternoon of February 9, 1942, workmen in the former grand salon were preparing to cut down the last of four metal stanchions that had once supported glass fountains of light. To do so, they had cleared a space among the sea of burlap-covered bales of kapok-filled lifejackets. (Kapok is both buoyant and highly inflammable.) While one man worked with the acetylene torch, a girdle of sheet metal protected the floor and a sheet of asbestos kept sparks from reaching the bales. But owing to a communications breakdown, no firewatchers were on duty and the two buckets of water nearby in case a spark escaped sat unattended. Just as the man with the welding torch was getting down to work, a couple of sailors sauntered into the lounge and began playing the grand piano. Elsewhere in the room, men in shirtsleeves were laying sheets of linoleum. First one, then the second, of the stanchion's three legs was burned through and work had started on the third. When someone yelled "Fire!" it was already too late. (Continued on page 183)

This page and overleaf: *On February 9, 1942, workmen in the Normandie's grand salon inadvertently set fire to a bale of life preservers. The blaze raced through the ship but, miraculously, almost no one was seriously hurt. By the time the fire had been brought under*

control too much water had been pumped into the ship, causing her to list beyond the point of no return. The mooring lines snapped and she wallowed onto her side.

Were it not for the scale of the tragedy that followed, the whole thing might have seemed comical. Almost everything that could go wrong did. The nearest fire hose, rescued from beneath a pile of bales, yielded a bucketful of water, then dribbled dry. In no time, the bales of lifejackets were ablaze, yet no one could find the fire alarm. It wouldn't have helped anyway, since it had been disconnected. So had the ship's direct line to the New York Fire Department, which wasn't alerted until twelve minutes after the first flames appeared. The ship's own main fire station had been moved but didn't yet possess a telephone. Soon the grand salon was a roaring inferno and the blaze was spreading. When the New York fire trucks finally arrived, the firemen were delayed in getting on board the ship by the streams of workmen pouring off, many of them choking from the smoke they had inhaled. Remarkably, of the more than three thousand on board—more than had ever sailed on a transatlantic voyage—only two fatalities resulted from the fire.

Ironically, had the *Normandie* simply been evacuated and left to burn, she might have been better off. By 6:00 p.m. the fire was out, but the great ship had developed a perilous list to port, away from the pier. Fireboats working alongside her had poured much more water into the hull than the land-based firetrucks, creating a portside list. Cargo doors left open did the rest. During the night, the ship leaned ever more dangerously away from the pier. Then the mooring lines snapped, and the pride of the French Line wallowed onto her side.

There she lay for eighteen months while six separate investigations sought to apportion the blame and the Navy tried to decide what to do with her. In those dark days, as the advancing Japanese juggernaut rolled from conquest to conquest in the Pacific, the *Normandie* acquired a potent symbolism. "It was as if the Empire State Building had slowly teetered and fallen sideways into the street," wrote one

Below: *An interior shot of the fire-ravaged* Normandie *after salvaging shows the staircase leading to the café grill, a striking contrast to its original hauteur (inset).* **Opposite:** *The stages of the Normandie's capsizing.*

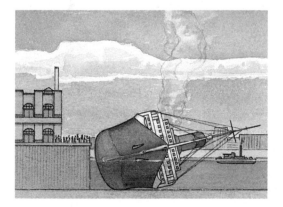

American journalist. Finally the navy concluded that she was worth more alive than dead and that they could turn her salvage into a public-relations triumph that would undo some of the damage done by the fire while providing a salvage school for the navy divers soon to be needed in the invasion of Europe. Perhaps she would make a troopship yet.

The navy got its ship back, but the victory was a Pyrrhic one. The greatest salvage operation in history took sixteen months of painstaking, backbreaking work in unbelievable conditions at a cost of $4.74 million, but by September 1943 the *Normandie* was once more afloat. In early November, she was towed to drydock in the Brooklyn Navy Yard, only to reveal that the damage to her hull made refitting prohibitively expensive. She spent the remainder of the war as an empty hulk tied to a Brooklyn pier. After the war, when the French government expressed no interest in reacquiring her, she was sold for scrap.

By then her famous fittings had been auctioned off and scattered to the four winds. Some are in private collections, others in the most unlikely of public places. *La Paix*, the tall, slender statue that gazed so nobly on the worshipers in the first-class dining room, now presides over a Long Island cemetery. The ship's other major statue, *La Normandie*, the earthy peasant girl formerly dominating the stairs leading from the café grill to the smoking room, now surveys the bar of the Fontainebleau Hotel in Miami Beach. Two sets of bronze doors, with medallions representing the cities of Normandy, which once formed the entrance to the main dining room, have for many years graced the front and side entrances of Our Lady of Lebanon Church in Brooklyn. A portion of *The Chariot of Poseidon*, one of the four monumental glass reliefs that decorated the grand salon, now hangs in the cafeteria of the Metropolitan Museum of Art. At Mr. Chow's Restaurant on East 47th Street in New York City, you can use some of the *Normandie*'s Christofle silverware and admire the lacquered-wood doors displaying vividly colored jungle scenes that formerly hung between the smoking room and the grand salon.

Of all the great lost liners, *Normandie*'s fate may be the saddest, a high-society life cut off before its prime. Better to have sunk at sea and remained intact in memory and in fact than to have died such a slow, ignoble death.

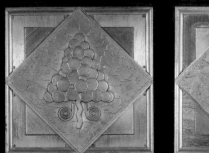 

Above: *Two gilded bronze panels that originally flanked the doors to the first-class dining room.*
Below: *The upholstered chairs from the grand salon bore a pattern from Aubusson tapestry.*
Right: *The legs of a sea nymph from one of the lacquered panels in the grand salon.*

Mementos of the *Normandie*

Left: An elegant chrome vase bearing the logo of the Compagnie Générale Transatlantique.

Above: In this postcard of the Deauville Suite, a similar silver vase has pride of place.

Top right: Various first-class artifacts, including a silver table number, a telephone and three ashtrays.

Middle right: A first-class suite, featuring one of Normandie's distinctive vases and a similar telephone.

Far right: A souvenir clock given to passengers on the Normandie's maiden voyage.

Bottom right: A Normandie perfume bottle, specially created by the Paris designer Patou, also for the maiden voyage.

After World War II, the
transatlantic passenger ship
entered its last golden age. But the
heyday was short-lived. By the late
fifties, fast and comfortable jet
airplane travel attracted an
increasing share of the transatlantic
trade. The loss of the *Andrea Doria*
off Nantucket in the summer of
1956 seems in retrospect to have
sounded the death knell of a whole
way of traveling.

First light on the morning of
July 26, 1956, revealed the now-derelict
Andrea Doria awaiting her inevitable end.

Fast Fade

The Twilight of the Atlantic Passenger Liner, 1945~1956

Opposite: The Queen Elizabeth's first peacetime departure from Southampton on October 16, 1946, was cause for national pride and local celebration. Top: The Queen Mary soon resumed her regular sailings to New York. Above: With the Queen Elizabeth joining her, Cunard now had its long-awaited two-ship service.

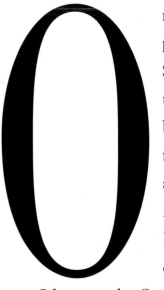

O n October 16, 1946, a great ocean liner pulled away from her pier in Southampton to begin her maiden voyage to New York. Slightly longer and with marginally more gross tonnage than the *Queen Mary*, the younger ship bore a clear family resemblance. But with her bow angled forward and only two huge funnels instead of three, she presented a racier, more modern appearance than her predecessor. She was Cunard's *Queen Elizabeth*, symbol to the crowds who waved her off that day of Britain's maritime resurgence in the difficult times following the end of World War II.

Of course, the *Queen Elizabeth* was not really a new ship and this was not her first voyage to America. Following her secret dash to New York in 1940, she had joined the *Queen Mary* as one of the two troopships nonpareil, whose joint accomplishment in ferrying Canadian and American servicemen to Europe had, in Churchill's estimation, shortened the conflict by a year. But until now she had never sailed in civilian garb, with her funnels, painted Cunard's trademark orange and black, rising from a gleaming white superstructure. Belowdecks, the grime and graffiti left by hundreds of thousands of soldier-passengers had been scrubbed away and painted over to bring her public rooms and private quarters up to the level expected of a luxury liner on the transatlantic run.

On this first commercial voyage, every berth was filled, and the passenger list included the Russian foreign ministers Molotov and Vishinsky, traveling to the first session of the newly formed United Nations. Her commander, Commodore Sir James Bissett, was at the peak of a career that had begun in the dying days of sail. As second officer on board the *Carpathia* in 1912, he had played a supporting role in the rescue of the survivors of the *Titanic* disaster. During World War II, he had commanded with distinction the same ship he now directed in peacetime.

There would be no speed records on this maiden crossing, nor any sought. In a climate of postwar shortages, there was no sense burning unnecessary oil, explained Commodore Bissett. The third day out, an autumn gale slowed the ship down and kept many passengers in their cabins, but the voyage was otherwise uneventful. The greatest suspense surrounded the threat of a dock strike in New York. Would the ship be diverted to Halifax or would Captain Bissett attempt a docking without the aid of tugs? The strike evaporated in the heat of disapproving public opinion, and the *Queen Elizabeth* arrived on schedule on October 21, the perfect herald of a return to transatlantic normalcy.

Although there were boom years to come, nothing would ever be quite the same again on the North Atlantic, because ships no longer held a passenger monopoly. For most of the 1930s, the only challenge had come from the German airships *Graf Zeppelin* and *Hindenburg*, which had inaugurated the first nonstop air service between Europe and North America. By the end of the decade, British and American flying boats made the transatlantic run, but they were expensive and required multiple stops for refueling. The war had speeded the development of the long-range airplane capable of ferrying passengers nonstop across the ocean in reasonable comfort in less than a day. Even the fastest ships took five days from port to port. Inevitably, as airplanes flew faster and became more comfortable, more and more travelers chose them over ocean liners.

Yet the postwar decade was a busy time on the North Atlantic, due to the flood of businessmen and tourists traveling between North America and Europe. After the refurbished *Queen Mary* returned to the Atlantic run in the summer of 1947, Cunard finally had its two-ship service. In the next few years, the company enjoyed record profits while dominating a market of mostly aging prewar ships that included the company's

In the wake of the war, American businessmen traveled frequently to a rebuilding Europe, and tourists returned in droves. It was a period when Cunard could still boast about traveling by passenger ship that "getting there is half the fun," an idea the pictures (opposite and above) in the company's brochures played up.

Far right: *Germany's prewar* Europa *was reborn as France's* Liberté, *but not before she sank in Le Havre harbor and had to be expensively salvaged.*

own venerable *Aquitania*, commissioned back in 1914.

Despite the writing in the sky, splendid new ships entered service in the 1950s, though none rivaled the prewar superliners in size or pretension. Undoubtedly the greatest among them was the *United States*, a marvel of the shipbuilder's art and the fastest ocean liner ever built. William Francis Gibbs, America's leading naval architect, had dreamed of something like her almost since boyhood, but had been thwarted in his ambition by his country's unwillingness to truly enter the

"LIBERTÉ"

Atlantic sweepstakes. After World War I, Gibbs had directed the refitting of the *Leviathan* (formerly the *Vaterland*) for peacetime use. And in the late thirties, he'd been handed the commission to design the *America*, the largest American ship to date. But only with the *United States* was he given virtual free rein to build the finest ship possible.

This freedom came from the involvement of the United States Navy, which, following the great success of the two British Queens in wartime, coveted a big passenger ship that could easily be converted into a trooper. The navy ended up subsidizing 70 percent of the *United States*' astonishing $78 million price tag. Easy convertibility partly accounted for the simplicity of her decor—in some eyes rather cold and sterile—but the other reason was Gibbs's obsession with fire prevention. (He had also designed the most powerful fire pumper ever.) The *United States* was a ship of steel, glass, fireproof synthetics—and aluminum. Gibbs even tried to persuade Steinway to provide an

Opposite above left: *The SS United States,* *the fastest passenger ship ever built, departs from her New York pier.* Opposite right: *The United States'* *interiors lacked the warmth of earlier passenger liners. But her dining room (top) and her first-class staterooms (middle) offered luxury and comfort. Obsessed with fire prevention, her builder, William Francis Gibbs (bottom), used no flammable materials in the new ship.* Above right: *The United States* *arrives off New York's Ambrose Lightship at the close of her record-breaking round-trip maiden voyage in 1952.*

aluminum piano, but the company absolutely refused. By slightly stretching the truth, the United States Lines could claim that the only wood on the new ship was found in the piano and the butcher block. This is not to say that Gibbs stinted on passenger comfort. Among her many amenities, the *United States* was the world's first completely air-conditioned liner.

Gibbs's greatest accomplishment, however, resided in the *United States'* speed. From the moment she was launched, she had the look of a racer. "Even at rest, the ship seemed to strain at the leash," writes John Maxtone-Graham. But it was her remarkable power plant, including the most powerful turbines yet built, that enabled her to reach the speed of 38.25 knots during trials. (The true figure was kept secret for many years, as were details of her hull design and propulsion system.) On her maiden voyage in 1952, she made the *Bremen's* 1929 besting of the *Mauretania's* mark look slightly tame. Her eastbound passage from the Ambrose Lightship to Bishop's rock lasted only three days, ten hours and forty minutes, ten hours faster than the *Queen Mary* had ever managed.

Despite her interior austerity, the *United States* became a very popular ship—even with wealthy travelers—favored by among others the Duke and Duchess of Windsor. As almost always in the past, the speed prize paid dividends. Nor did it hurt that she was the only American superliner at a time when Americans dominated the passenger lists and were ascendant in almost every technological sphere. But she was also a no-nonsense ship in a no-nonsense time, without the vast public rooms—extra hull subdivisions for safety eliminated these—that had characterized the great ships between the wars.

By the mid-1950s, with the postwar passenger boom at its peak, more than fifty passenger liners sailed the sealanes between Europe and America. Among the most splendid were two new ships of the Italian Line, the *Cristoforo Colombo* and the *Andrea Doria*. They were built for luxury, not speed, and to take advantage of the sunnier southern route. The *Andrea Doria* was the first liner to possess three outdoor swimming pools, one each for first, cabin and tourist class. Her lines were graceful, her public rooms lavishly decorated and crowded with artworks and her most desirable first-class suites as rarefied as any that had come before. She was a superb expression of her time and nationality, a ship that combined fifties' modernity with a keen awareness of Italy's extraordinary artistic heritage. As the Italian Line's flagship, the first Italian trans-atlantic steamship launched since World War II, she was in her own way as much a symbol of national pride as had been the *Normandie*.

She was also equipped with the latest in navigational equipment, including two sets of radar, the still-developing technology that had transformed the maritime battle-fields of World War II and was now standard equipment in the merchant marine. But even if the radar failed and somehow a collision happened, the *Andrea Doria* was in theory unsinkable. Her eleven watertight compartments were so constructed that she would remain afloat if any two were breached—more than that her builders could not imagine—and so that she would never take on a list of more than fifteen degrees. As an extra safety precaution, her lifeboats could still be launched if the list reached twenty degrees. Yet the *Andrea Doria* was destined to become the last great lost ship of

Above: *The bow of the* Cristoforo Colombo *was virtually identical to that of her older sister, the* Andrea Doria. Below: *The bridge of the* Andrea Doria. Opposite: *The* Andrea Doria *was justifiably considered one of the most beautiful ships of the postwar era. She was named after a sixteenth-century Genoese admiral, whose statue gazed out over the first-class lounge.*

a transatlantic passenger era that was about to fade away.

Her story provides vivid evidence that "despite all the safety gadgets, the mind is supreme and the mind is fallible." The quotation belongs to Harry Manning, first captain of the record-breaking *United States*, reflecting on the collision between the *Andrea Doria* and the *Stockholm*. The same words could equally have been written following the loss of the *Titanic* or the *Empress of Ireland*. Add to human frailty a goodly portion of bad luck, and the collision that led to the sinking takes on the kind of inevitability that prompted William Hoffer in his book *Saved!* to comment that "the two ships seemed drawn together by a magnet of fate." And despite many hours of testimony after the accident and much analysis, no one will ever be completely sure precisely how it happened.

We do know that on the evening of July 25, 1956, two passenger ships were converging on a point southwest of the Nantucket Lightship, which marks the entry to and exit from the crowded approach to New York harbor. The 697-foot-long *Andrea Doria*, carrying a nearly full complement of 1,706 passengers and crew, was nearing the end of a mostly sunny and uneventful nine-day voyage from Genoa to New York. The *Stockholm*, at 528 feet in length and only 12,165 tons, one of the smallest of the new postwar liners, was just beginning its homeward voyage to Sweden. On the *Andrea Doria*'s bridge, overseeing the work of the two senior officers on the watch, stood fifty-eight-year-old Captain Piero Calamai, a veteran of thirty-nine years at sea and hundreds of Atlantic crossings. On the bridge of the *Stockholm*, the ship's youthful third officer, twenty-six-year-old Johan-Ernst Bogislaus Carstens-Johannsen, was in charge of the 8:30 to 12:00 p.m. watch. It was standard policy in the Swedish Line, as on most liners, for only one officer and two seamen to stand each bridge watch.

At 10:20 p.m., the *Andrea Doria* came abeam of the Nantucket Lightship, and Captain Calamai ordered a new course that aimed directly at the Ambrose Lightship, which marks the mouth of New York harbor. The two ships were now approaching on roughly parallel courses, but being still beyond the range of each other's radar were as yet unaware of each other's presence. To complicate matters, the *Andrea Doria* was steaming in fog, while the *Stockholm* sailed through a clear night bathed in moonlight. Carstens-Johannsen had no inkling of the fogbank that lay just ahead.

Opposite top: *The* Andrea Doria *passes the Statue of Liberty at the end of her maiden voyage in January 1953.*
Opposite middle: *Three weeks before her sinking, the* Andrea Doria *departed New York for the last time.*
Opposite bottom: *A dramatic view of the Manhattan skyline with the* Andrea Doria*'s bowdeck in the foreground.*

Given the circumstances, neither ship was exercising maximum caution. Since mid-afternoon, the *Andrea Doria* had been steaming through patchy fog, at times dense enough to make the bow invisible from the bridge, but Captain Calamai had reduced speed only a little. He had a schedule to keep, and he was confident that his radar would alert him in ample time to avoid any problems. He had, however, ordered various standard fog precautions: a lookout was posted in the bow and the watertight doors were closed.

The *Stockholm* had as yet no reason to reduce speed, but every reason to expect fog in the waters south of Nantucket Island, where the cold Labrador Current encounters the warm Gulf Stream. Furthermore, the ship was traveling to the north of the recommended outbound route on a course likely to bring it into contact with incoming ships in one of the busiest sealanes in the world. (Many outgoing ships spurned the recommended route twenty miles south of the Nantucket Lightship because it added distance and time.) Yet Captain H. Gunnar Nordenson saw no reason to join his third officer on the bridge. Third Officer Carstens-Johannsen (known to his crewmates as Carstens) was perfectly capable of navigating the ship, even in these treacherous waters, as long as the weather stayed clear.

The *Andrea Doria*, whose radar had a slightly greater range than the *Stockholm*'s, detected an oncoming ship at about 10:45 p.m., at a distance of about seventeen nautical miles. Curzio Franchini, the ship's second officer, alerted the captain, and Calamai immediately requested the other ship's bearing. She was only four degrees off the starboard bow—in other words, almost dead ahead. This information didn't worry the *Andrea Doria*'s captain or the two watch officers on the bridge. There was ample time and distance to pass the oncoming vessel with plenty of room. They had done so a thousand times before with a thousand other ships. Only one important decision needed to be made—whether to pass the ship to port or starboard. According to Franchini, the oncoming ship continued to bear slightly to the right, causing Captain Calamai to begin to think it was a small coastal vessel that would soon turn north to Nantucket.

On board the *Stockholm*, Third Officer Carstens saw things quite differently. He had just picked up a blip on his radar indicating a ship twelve nautical miles away and slightly to his port. Acting according to standard Swedish Line procedure, he plotted the course of the oncoming vessel, which required two radar fixes. By the time he'd completed his calculations, the other ship was fewer than six miles away. It appeared set to pass to the north, but by less than a mile. As soon as the other ship came into view, Carstens told himself, he would alter course to starboard, so as to increase the width of their passing distance. After several minutes, he began to wonder why the other ship's lights did not appear. He could still see the moon, and the possibility he was sailing into a fogbank seems never to have occurred to him.

Those navigating the two ships racing toward each other at a combined speed of roughly 40 knots had somehow come to opposite conclusions. Aboard the *Andrea Doria*, the approaching ship seemed to be maintaining a position just off the starboard bow. According to the *Stockholm*'s radar, the other vessel seemed clearly to be a few degrees to port and on a parallel course. One of the radar sets, or one of the men who read them, was wrong. Given the state of radar at that time and the fact that no ship keeps a perfect, steady course, small errors can be exaggerated. On board the *Andrea Doria*, such an error might have been caught, had someone bothered to plot the oncoming ship's course instead of relying on an eyeball estimate from the radar screen, but on the Italian Line such calculations were not routine practice. The men in command on both ships seem to have had more faith in their radar—and their ability to interpret it—than they should have.

This faith led Captain Calamai to make one of his most controversial decisions of the night. He decided to pass the approaching vessel starboard side to starboard side. Standard procedure when two ships meet at sea is for a port-side-to-port-side passing, but the *Andrea Doria*'s skipper thought he had good reasons for making an exception. The other ship was already to starboard—or so he believed. A port-side passing would mean crossing her bow and sailing closer to more heavily traveled coastal waters. Given the wide and empty ocean to his left, it seemed natural to stay to port and stay clear. About 11:05 p.m., with the other ship about three and a half nautical miles away, Captain Calamai ordered a small four-degree course change to port to increase the passing distance. Neither ship had yet seen the other, except on radar.

Just as the *Andrea Doria* changed course, the two ships finally made visual contact. Only two miles now separated them, a perilously short distance, given their combined

Because she traveled the warmer southern transatlantic route and traversed the western half of the Mediterranean, the Andrea Doria *boasted three outdoor pools and ample outdoor deckspace for recreation or relaxation.*

A first-class stateroom on the Andrea Doria *displays the trappings of 1950s modernity. By now comfort and luxury went hand in hand. In first-class cabins a private bathroom was standard and the whole ship was air conditioned.*

speed. They were converging at a slight angle, so that the *Andrea Doria* saw lights to its right and the *Stockholm* lights to its left. Thus the first sight of the other ship only reinforced the false assumptions on each bridge: the other vessel was where it was expected.

On the *Stockholm*'s bridge, Carstens now issued an order he might more wisely have given long before—a sharp turn to starboard to give the oncoming ship a wider berth. Unfortunately for him, Captain Calamai remained convinced the *Stockholm* would pass him safely starboard to starboard. Without realizing it, Carstens was turning his ship *toward* the *Andrea Doria*'s course. And he failed to signal his turn with the usual blasts on the ship's whistle. Then the bridge telephone rang and he turned away to answer it.

For a split second, Captain Calamai couldn't believe what he was seeing. With the approaching ship only a mile away, its masthead lights had finally materialized clearly enough from the fog for him to visually determine its course. He watched intently as the lower navigation light crossed from right to left in front of the higher one. The other ship was turning right! Then the red light appeared, indicating the ship was showing its port side, confirming the worst. Third Officer Eugenio Giannini had seen it too. "She is turning, she is turning!" he shouted. "She is coming toward us!"

All thirty-nine of Captain Calamai's years at sea must have passed in front of his eyes in the instant before he called out his next order. Had experience prepared him for this his greatest test? "*Tutto sinistra*," he called out. "Full left." He would put his faith in the *Andrea Doria*'s speed and maneuverability, hoping to turn left faster than the other ship was turning right. But a huge ocean liner going nearly full speed doesn't turn on a dime.

On board the *Stockholm*, Carstens brought his gaze back from the bridge telephone, still assuming all ahead of him was fine. On the phone had been the crow's-nest lookout telling him what he already knew: the lights of a ship were visible twenty degrees to port. Carstens had turned away just as the other ship began its hard left turn. Now it took him a few moments to grasp what was happening. The stranger was turning across his bow! He wrenched the handle of the engine telegraph to full astern and shouted to his helmsman, "Hard-a-starboard!" It was too little, too late.

Had Captain Calamai turned right instead of left, he might well have avoided a collision or minimized its impact. A glancing blow head to head is less damaging than a broadside ramming, but that is what the *Andrea Doria* received. The bow of the

Stockholm plunged into the Italian liner's starboard hull plates just aft of her bridge, ripping open seven of her eleven decks, the hole reaching almost down to her keel. For a moment, the smaller ship lodged there like a stopper in a bottle, then the force of the water rushing past the *Andrea Doria*'s hull—she was still moving at almost full speed—tore the *Stockholm* away. A torrent of seawater began to pour through the gaping hole in the Italian liner's hull. The time was just past 11:10 p.m.

With the *Andrea Doria* scheduled to dock in New York early the following morning, many of the ship's 1,134 passengers, especially those with young children, had already retired. But the moment of collision caught quite a few passengers engaged in final-night entertainments. The dance band in the first-class Belvedere Room nightclub had launched into yet another rendition of "Arrividerci, Roma," when it literally tumbled off its podium amid a clatter of instruments as dancing couples toppled to the floor. In the tourist-class dining room, where passengers were enjoying a Jane Russell movie called *Foxfire*, the screen went dead and a short-lived panic erupted in the darkness. Throughout the ship, those who hadn't yet gone to bed rushed to their staterooms, woke sleeping children, grabbed life jackets and a few belongings, then headed for their muster stations. For within minutes of the impact, the *Andrea Doria* had taken on an alarming list to starboard.

Those passengers already in their cabins when the collision happened fared very differently, depending on where their quarters were located. On the port side, the worst experience was to be thrown out of bed or off one's feet. Fourteen-year-old Madge Young, who was brushing her teeth in the bathroom of her first-class stateroom on the portside upper deck heard "a terrible crash" and then fell into the bathtub with no harm done. But in cabin 56 on the starboard side, in which the Young family had originally been booked, Thure Peterson actually glimpsed the *Stockholm*'s hull slide past him before he lost consciousness. When he came to, he discovered his wife, Martha, trapped beneath a pile of wreckage. (Despite heroic efforts to free her by Peterson and a steward named Giovanni Rovelli and the ministrations of Dr. Bruno Tortari Donati, Mrs. Peterson eventually died from her injuries.)

In retrospect, some escapes seemed miraculous but none more than that of fourteen-year-old Linda Morgan, whose mother was trapped in cabin 54. Asleep in cabin 52,

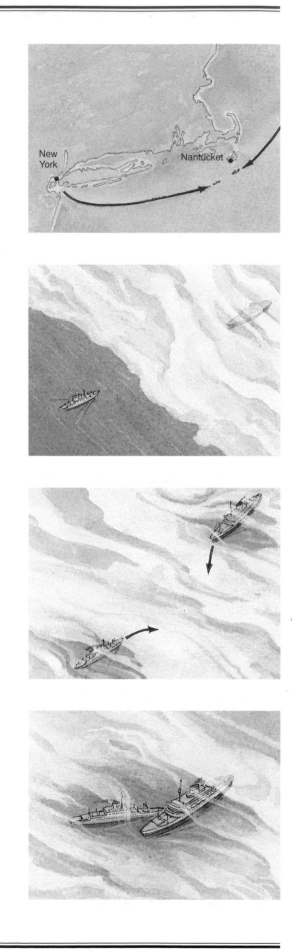

Opposite: *On the evening of July 25, 1956, the* Andrea Doria *was New York-bound off Massachusetts while the* Stockholm *was beginning her run for Europe. A fog bank shrouded the* Andrea Doria *while the* Stockholm *sailed under clear night skies. The two ships were converging on a point just west of the Nantucket Lightship. Misjudging each other's course and intentions, both ships turned into the other's path. By the time they saw each other, it was too late.*
Below: *Linda Morgan went to sleep on the* Andrea Doria *and woke up on the* Stockholm.
Bottom: *Passengers wait on the* Stockholm's *deck.*
Overleaf: *The* Andrea Doria *sinking.*

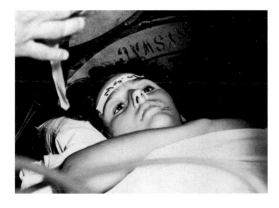

only two doors down from the Petersons, Linda had somehow been catapulted out of her bed and onto the *Stockholm*'s crushed bow, where a crewman heard her calling for her mama, with whom she was eventually reunited. (The sister sleeping in the bed next to her was killed instantly.) Journalists later dubbed Linda Morgan "the miracle girl."

One passenger on the starboard side just aft of the area of the collision articulated what must have been on many minds. Mrs. Richardson Dilworth awoke to find her husband, the mayor of Philadelphia, on the floor between their beds. She had recently read Walter Lord's best-selling account of the *Titanic* sinking, *A Night to Remember*. "I think we have hit an iceberg like the *Titanic*," she told him. She was clearly wrong on one count. Icebergs don't make it as far south as Nantucket. Whether the fate of the *Andrea Doria* would resemble that of the *Titanic* remained an open question as the ship's list grew sharper.

Within a few minutes of the collision, the list exceeded twenty degrees, a point beyond which the system of watertight compartments was compromised. At least one and as many as three of these were open to the sea, and any list beyond fifteen degrees meant water would spill forward and aft. On the bridge, Captain Calamai knew only that his ship was doomed, but not how long she would stay afloat. He probably realized, however, why the list was so sudden and extreme. The *Stockholm* had pierced the *Andrea Doria*'s hull in the worst possible place, punching through starboard fuel tanks, empty this late in the voyage, that lay deep in the compartment just forward of the generator room. As water poured into the starboard tanks, the buoyancy of the undamaged port-side tanks—also empty—exacerbated an already bad situation. To make matters worse, some commentators also believe that the ship's builders had neglected to install a watertight door in the tunnel providing access from the generator room to the fuel tanks. Water rushed through this tunnel into the generator space, making the watertight bulkhead meaningless.

Since the ship seemed likely to capsize before rescue could arrive, Captain Calamai quickly took steps to organize the evacuation of the *Andrea Doria* by lifeboat. But the crew dispatched to swing out the port-side boats discovered that the ship's list now exceeded the maximum angle that allowed them to do so. A surfeit of lifeboats had suddenly become a shortage. Fully loaded, the starboard side boats could carry only

1,004 of the 1,706 on board. This grim echo of the *Titanic*'s predicament may explain why Calamai never sounded the abandon-ship signal. Perhaps he feared a panic.

In the end, the remarkable rescue of all of the *Andrea Doria*'s passengers not killed as a result of the initial collision owed more to good luck than to the leadership of her captain or the comportment of her crew: though many behaved admirably and some heroically, many others did not. The first boats did not leave the ship until more than an hour after the collision, and these were packed with more crew than passengers. When the boats reached the *Stockholm*, which soon dispatched boats of its own to aid the sinking liner, few aboard them volunteered to return for others. Most of the first- and cabin-class passengers aboard the *Andrea Doria* waited for almost three hours at their muster stations without any word from the ship's commander. In tourist class, matters nearly got out of hand. Many of the passengers lodged in the lowest areas of the ship had to fight their way through torrents of oily seawater in order to reach the deck. For some it took ninety minutes to make the nightmarish ascent.

The arrival of the lady of the hour sounded a noble echo from an earlier era. This was the liner *Ile de France*, the art-deco precursor of the late lamented *Normandie*, captained by Baron Raoul de Beaudéan. When Captain de Beaudéan picked up the *Andrea Doria*'s distress signal, he turned his liner around and steamed for the distress position. By the time he reached the *Andrea Doria* at about 2:00 a.m., the *Ile de France* was as prepared to handle the survivors as had been Captain Rostron's *Carpathia* more than forty years earlier. With the ultimate in panache and seamanship, Beaudéan brought his huge liner to rest a mere four hundred yards away—the fog had conveniently cleared just in time. And, though other ships on the scene, including the *Stockholm*, took off many passengers, it was the *Ile de France* that rescued by far the greatest share.

At first Captain Calamai refused to leave his ship, even after he thought the last passenger and most of the crew had departed. (Unknown to him, third-class passenger Robert Hudson was still in the ship's hospital. On painkillers for a back injury, he slept through the collision and the evacuation, but was rescued by a passing lifeboat.) Calamai still hoped she could be towed to safety before she sank, and he wanted to remain on board until the tugs arrived. Even when the list reached a calamitous forty degrees, he preferred to stay; he would go down with his ship, if necessary. He ordered

Top: By dawn, the last of the Andrea Doria's passengers had been evacuated and Captain Calamai had finally been persuaded to abandon his ship. But he still hoped it might be towed to safety. Below and right: As the ship began its final plunge, most of the port lifeboats were torn free, but some went down with the ship.

Above: **Boston Herald** *photographer Harold Trask, who arrived on the scene just in time to record the sinking, won a Pulitzer Prize for his chronicle of the ship's last moments. For fifteen minutes following the sinking, a 700-foot-long swath of bubbles turned the sea a bright green.*
Right: *The* **Stockholm's** *bow was crushed, but she remained firmly afloat.*

the remaining crew to abandon ship, but they refused to leave without him. And so, reluctantly, just as dawn was breaking, he stepped into a lifeboat. It was just past 5:30 a.m.

The *Andrea Doria* finally capsized and sank at 10:09 a.m. on July 26, eleven hours after the collision had taken place, while chartered planes carrying news photographers recorded the event for posterity. (The *Stockholm*, her bow staved in but her hull still seaworthy, made it back to New York under her own steam. After repairs, she returned to the Atlantic service.) Only 46 of the 1,706 passengers and crew perished in the sinking or its aftermath, almost all of them as result of injuries sustained in the initial collision. Five crewmen from the *Stockholm* also lost their lives. But it could so easily have been much worse. If the *Andrea Doria* had sunk as fast as Captain Calamai and his officers at first had feared there would have been a catastrophe on a *Titanic* scale.

The *Andrea Doria* sank while ocean travel still enjoyed a postwar boom. Yet only two years later, this boom was turning rapidly to bust. In 1958, the Boeing 707 inaugurated nonstop jet service between North America and Europe. Two years later, airplanes had almost 70 percent of the transatlantic passenger business. Within a decade, the figure would be more like 95 percent. As the number of ocean travelers dropped precipitously, more and more ships were withdrawn from service. And those ships that stubbornly clung to their old ways often traveled more empty than full. On one winter crossing in the 1960s, the *Queen Elizabeth* carried 200 passengers and 1,200 crew.

A few great new ships were built, but with the exception of the *France* of 1962, these vessels were never intended exclusively as transatlantic carriers. Instead they spent much of the year cruising in warmer climes, making regular Atlantic crossings only during the summer tourist season. The last and most enduring of these superliners was the *Queen Elizabeth 2*, which flourishes to this day. It seems appropriate that during the summer months, passengers still flock to cross the Atlantic in a Cunard ship laid down in the same yards that built the *Lusitania* and the *Queen Mary*, and that Cunard, the first regularly scheduled Atlantic carrier, has become the last.

Exploring the *Andrea Doria*

T he day I visited the *Andrea Doria* the visibility was so bad that we landed *NR-1* on the wreck's port side like a plane making an instrument landing in dense fog. At least we proved to the navy that their small nuclear sub could safely touch down on a sunken hull, as we hoped to do on our expedition to the *Britannic* later the same year. But by far the clearest images of the *Doria* have come from photographs taken by scuba divers.

Like the *Empress of Ireland*, the *Andrea Doria* lies within reach of serious divers, but it is not a place for the faint of heart. The ship lies on her side at a depth of about 250 feet in an area where the underwater weather can change suddenly from clear and calm to a ripping current filled with sediment. Fishing nets drape the hull, but even more treacherous is the invisible web of

Above and right: *The* Andrea Doria *at the time of her sinking in July 1956 and as she looks today.*

tough monofilament fishing line in which fins or tanks can easily become caught. In the warren of cold, dark rooms and corridors that form the dead ship's interior, a diver can easily become hopelessly lost. And then there are the sharks.

But the reward for those who venture this deep is to briefly rediscover a ship still recognizably the luxury liner that gaily cruised the southern Atlantic route in the 1950s. Most of the deck hardware and all three swimming pools are clearly visible. Lifeboat davits still jut from the boat deck and great cranes dominate the bow. The ship's name can still be made out on both the bow and stern.

On a sunny day when the visibility is good, a diver can swim along inside the portside promenade deck, gazing through windows at the luminous bright green "sky" above. At the stern the great bronze port propeller encrusted with sea anemones looms dramatically out of the underwater darkness. Many divers venture inside the ship through "Gimbel's Hole," the opening cut by Peter Gimbel in order to retrieve the ship's safe. Once inside many visit the dining room or the gift shop, both now emptied of anything worth salvaging.

After twenty minutes exploring the wreck, the diver must spend another ninety decompressing before returning to the surface. But he brings back with him unforgettable images of ruined luxe and of the end of a magnificent era in ocean travel.

Opposite: *This bell remained in place on the* Andrea Doria*'s stern until the late 1980s.*
Above right: *Divers scraped away marine growth to reveal an embossed* A *from the ship's name on the stern.*
Right: *Fishing nets are among the wreck's many hazards.*

Left and below: *One of the ship's shuffle board courts then and now.*
Right and far right: *The first-class cocktail bar then and now.*

Left and right: *A second-class stateroom then, with built-in washbasin, and a similar washbasin today.*

Above and left: *Earlier salvagers left Admiral Andrea Doria's feet when they took him from the first-class lounge. Now, they too are gone.*

Protecting Lost Liners

*The Emerging Law of Deep Ocean Discovery and the
Prospects for Creating Museums Beneath the Sea*

In late August of 1996, I followed the progress, with a mixture of fascination and dismay, of the salvagers attempting to raise a piece of hull plating from the *Titanic* debris field. Not that I was one of the seventeen hundred people who'd paid good money to witness this "historic" event from the comfort of one of the two luxury cruise ships that had sailed to the sinking site. I tracked the events on the high seas by way of the Internet, logging on each day to the website provided by the Discovery Channel, which was making a documentary about the expedition.

It was the fourth salvage expedition to a site that has by now been scoured in search of any artifact of arguable importance. But in the misleading news reports surrounding this latest enterprise, you would have thought the entire wreck of the *Titanic* was about to be lifted to the surface instead of a chunk of hull weighing about ten tons. The *Titanic*, characteristically, provided an appropriate degree of drama and suspense. From the beginning, the salvage operation was beset by technical difficulties. Plans for some dramatic filming of the wreck had to be abandoned. Although a small haul of artifacts, including a few bottles of Bass Ale for one of the expedition's sponsors, was salvaged, when the ten-ton slab of steel and rivets finally neared the surface, the cruise ships had already departed. They didn't miss anything. At the last minute, the cables that attached the floats to the salvaged section of the *Titanic*'s hull parted and it dropped back to the ocean bottom where it belongs. By the time you read these words, however, yet another salvage expedition may well have succeeded where the 1996 effort failed.

The *Titanic*'s salvagers argue that they are preserving for posterity pieces of a wreck that will otherwise decay into rubble, but this need not be the case. The technology for arresting the decline of this and other great lost ships already exists. We could clean the *Titanic*'s hull and repaint it underwater, if there was an agreement to maintain it the way we found it in 1985.

My opposition to the salvage of the *Titanic* and other important modern wrecks is well known, and I won't review my arguments here, but the fate of the *Titanic* since our 1985 discovery demonstrates the need for some sort of international agreement to govern the treatment of historically significant shipwrecks—whether they lie in the deep ocean or in more accessible shallow waters. What with the confusion between jurisdictions and the competing agendas of those interested in treasure and those determined to preserve history, the current situation borders on chaos.

Any wreck that lies within a country's twelve-mile territorial limit automatically becomes subject to the law of that country. Yet nations have seldom taken any interest in wrecks lying within their waters unless they represent an environmental risk or a hazard to shipping. The *Empress of Ireland*, a wreck of undoubted historical importance that rests in Canadian waters, lay unvisited for fifty years, and as far as I know, the Canadian government has never attempted to exercise jurisdiction over it. Since the late 1960s, however, the wreck has been visited by hundreds of scuba divers who have lifted uncounted artifacts, ranging from furniture to unopened champagne bottles, from the site. The two largest objects that have been brought to the surface are the bronze ship's bell and one of its propellers. (The propeller was subsequently sold for scrap.) Some visitors have even brought back bones belonging to the remains of the more than 400 bodies still entombed in the ship. (Divers refer to one particular part of the wreck as the boneyard.) But the worst damage has been done only recently, when a salvage company began ripping off the teak decking and reselling it at a big profit. This process left

Divers wrestle with a piece from the hull of the Titanic *during the unsuccessful 1996 attempt at bringing it to the surface.*

holes in the metal underdecking that admitted currents and microorganisms to parts of the wreck previously well preserved. When a local diver, who has led efforts to protect the wreck, went to court in an attempt to stop the salvage, he was denied any ownership over the *Empress of Ireland* site.

On the high seas, according to traditional salvage law, once a sunken ship has been abandoned by its original owner, it becomes fair game. (The only exception to this rule is a warship, which always remains the property of its country of origin.) The discoverer of a wreck can only stake a claim if he raises objects from the site, in which case an admiralty court can designate him the "salvor in possession." As long as the salvor works his claim, he maintains his exclusive rights to the wreck. In theory, then, RMS Titanic Inc, the salvor in possession of the *Titanic* wreck, could prevent the original discoverers from revisiting the site. At the very least, any attempt would likely lead to an interesting court case!

At least as far as shipwrecks lying in international waters are concerned, there are signs the traditional law of salvage is being superseded by a new law of deep-ocean discovery. The precedent-setting case revolved around the SS *Central America*, a side-paddle sailing steamer that sank 160 miles off the coast of South Carolina in September 1857 with 578 passengers and three tons of gold from the California gold fields aboard. When the Columbia-America Discovery Group found the wreck in

Above: *Part of the rich cargo of gold bars carried by the SS Central America, discovered in the summer of 1986.*
Far left: *One of the Central America's paddle wheels, whose power would have been boosted by sails whenever possible.*
Left: *A starfish perches atop a pile of gold coins.*

the summer of 1986, they laid claim to it on the basis of having visited the wreck site by means of remotely operated camera vehicles. They brought back no physical artifacts, only pictures.

After several years of legal wrangling, a Virginia district court awarded possession of the SS *Central America* to Columbus-America. As part of its decision, the court found that telepresence equals "telepossession." In other words, bringing back pictures has the legal weight of physical salvage. Just as important, however, was a claimant's commitment to treat the wreck with respect and to exploit it for more than mere commercial interest, "to act in good faith to preserve the scientific, historic, and, in limited situations where applicable, archaeological, provenance of the wreck and artifacts." Had we followed this legal route in 1985, we might well have been able to prevent the high-seas carnival that has unfolded at the *Titanic* wreck since then.

The emerging law of deep-ocean discovery won't protect wrecks lying in a country's territorial waters. Nor does it establish any ground rules for deciding when preservation of a wreck is preferable to salvage. To my mind, the ideal solution would be an international treaty that would govern the treatment of wrecks outside territorial limits and at least exert some moral suasion when a country deals with a wreck within its own waters. Such a treaty would need to set up a mechanism for deciding when a wreck is of truly historical importance or archeological value and would distinguish between a scientific explorer and a relic hunter. Ideally, an international commission with representatives from the scientific, historical, legal and salvage communities could arbitrate disputes over wrecks in the same way a local historical board decides whether an old building has historic value or can be safely torn down or altered.

With all the public interest that continues to surround the wreck of RMS *Titanic*, I'm hopeful that future deep-sea discoveries will be treated very differently.

The great lost liners will not live again and no traveling exhibit of salvaged artifacts will bring them back. The world that produced them, with its sharp class distinctions and its aristocracy of wealth and privilege, has long vanished. Passenger ships will never again be the "only way to cross."

One April soon after our discovery of the *Titanic*, I was invited by Cunard to join a voyage aboard the *Queen Elizabeth 2* intended to retrace the *Titanic*'s route. (Appropriately, icebergs forced us south of the actual course and caused us to put into Baltimore instead of New York.) It was a wonderful journey, including meals recreated from the actual menus of the maiden voyage. The *QE2* is certainly a magnificent ship, larger and more comfortable than the *Titanic*, with stabilizers that prevent much of the pitch and roll common in those earlier days. Unlike the vessels I'm used to, it was sometimes possible to forget I was on a ship at all. But the *QE2* resembles a modern resort hotel more than one of the great ocean liners built before World War II. Despite all the effort, I never felt very close to 1912.

I would love to sail on one of those great lost liners, to explore its unbelievable public rooms, hobnob with its rich and famous passengers, chat with a captain whose memories go back to the days of sail. I would love to eat its lavish meals served over many courses and be waited on by an attentive steward whose father and grandfather have gone to sea before him. But I can't. Probably the closest I have ever come is when visiting those extraordinary sunken ships—the *Lusitania*, the *Titanic* and the *Britannic*. They are the true inheritors of a world that is gone for good.

Acknowledgments

Rick Archbold wishes to thank the many people who contributed to the making of this book. Eric Sauder answered every question I posed, read the entire manuscript and made many helpful suggestions, especially in chapter two and in helping me restore some of the *Queen Mary's* neglected elegance. Simon Mills lent his expertise to the sections on the *Olympic, Titanic* and, above all, *Britannic.* (His book *HMHS Britannic: the Last Titan* was specially valuable.) John Maxtone-Graham read the manuscript and caught errors of both commission and omission.

Thanks, as always, to Ed and Karen Kamuda of the Titanic Historical Society for lending so freely from their archives and to Society historian Don Lynch for responding so quickly to my every request for help.

I was especially fortunate to find a liner buff and *Empress of Ireland* expert living in nearby Oakville, Ontario. Mark Reynolds not only let me borrow half the books in his liner library but helped me recreate a dive to the wreck today.

I'd also like to acknowledge the valuable help of the following: Sharon Gignac, who has transcribed every interview I've done with Bob Ballard; Graham Wignall, whose grandfather was a steamship stoker before the first war; Ken Marschall, who not only paints wonderful ships but lends out books from his private collection; Cathy Offinger, who can always find Bob Ballard, whether he's on land, in the air or beneath the sea; Father Roberto Pirrone, who is building a precise scale model of *Normandie;* Bill Sauder, who knows more than anyone else about the power plants on the *Lusitania* and *Mauretania;* Brian Skerry, who has made many dives to the wreck of the *Andrea Doria;* Anthony Walsh, the source for Percy Tyler's *Britannic* reminiscences; Rick Wrobol, for explicating the rules of deep-sea salvage.

And finally, my thanks to the team of professionals associated with Madison Press who take the words I write and place them in such beautiful settings: Ian Coutts, astute editor, indefatigable photo hunter and gifted comedian; Gord Sibley, long-suffering book designer; Sandra Hall, mistress of the production schedule and color approval; Hugh Brewster, master of both the big picture and the niggling detail.

Ken Marschall gives his thanks to Tom Nicolai, who lent him his large *Normandie* model and reference material, and to Vern Shrock, for his invaluable moral support and his willingness to help in any way possible to ensure the completion of these paintings.

Prints and posters of Ken Marschall's work are available from Trans-Atlantic Designs, P.O. Box 539, Redondo Beach, CA 90277, U.S.A. Telephone (310) 541-1246

Madison Press extends its thanks to Peter Christopher for his pictures of the White Swan Hotel, Paul Kubek for his shots in chapter five, and Philippe Beaudry, Gary Gentile and Brian Skerry for their underwater photography. Among those collectors not mentioned elsewhere, thanks to Carl House, Alan Hustak, Arnold Kludas, Stanley Lehrer, Gavin Murphy, Jack Shaum, and Ken Schultz, all of whom readily lent pictures and objects for use in this book. Thanks to John Provan for finding so many pictures of the great German liners. Dennis R. Kromm deserves special thanks for not only agreeing to have a Ken Marschall painting in his collection photographed but for arranging for the photography and the courier to send it to Madison. Thanks too to Angus Mitchell and John Fleming, for lending their family picture collections to Simon Mills who in turn lent them to Madison. Thanks also to D. Nigel Perkins, general manager of the White Swan Hotel in Alnwick, England, and D. J. Neal, site manager for Akzo Nobel Decorative Coatings, in Haltwhistle, both of whom granted permission to Peter Christopher to photograph *Olympic* interiors, and to F. Gregg Bemis for access to the *Lusitania* wreck.

For more information on *Titanic* and other liners of the past, readers should write the *Titanic Historical Society*, P.O. Box 51053, Indian Orchard, Massachusetts, 01151-0053 U.S.A.

Picture Credits

1 Deutsches Schiffahrtsmuseum.
2-3 Painting by Ken Marschall.
4-5 Painting by Ken Marschall.
6-7 Painting by Ken Marschall.
8 Left: Philippe Beaudry Collection.
8 Lower left: Eric Sauder Collection.
8 Right: Photograph courtesy of Christie's Images.
8-9 Hoover Institution, Stanford University.
9 Ken Marschall Collection.
10 Photograph by C.K. Peters, courtesy of Odyssey Corporation.
10-11 Photograph by C.K. Peters, courtesy of Odyssey Corporation.
12 Top: Photograph by C.K. Peters, courtesy of Odyssey Corporation.
12 Bottom: Photograph by C.K. Peters, courtesy of Odyssey Corporation.
13 Top: Photograph by C.K. Peters, courtesy of Odyssey Corporation.
13 Bottom: Photograph by C.K. Peters, courtesy of Odyssey Corporation.

Chapter One

14-15 Bridgeman Art Library, PFA 73338, Robert Dudley.
16-17 Mary Evans Picture Library.
18 Top: Mary Evans Picture Library.
18 Bottom (left to right) Mary Evans Picture Library.
19 Top: Mary Evans Picture Library.
19 Left: Maritime Museum of the Atlantic, MP 400.28.1.
20 Top: Maritime Museum of the Atlantic, MP 22.25.1.
20 Bottom: Eric Sauder Collection.
21 Left top: Eric Sauder Collection.
21 Left bottom: Eric Sauder Collection.
21 Right: *Savannah* by Carlton Chapman. Mariner's Museum, QO 231.
22-23 *Great Western Steamship Crossing the Atlantic* by H.E. Hudson. National Maritime Museum, photograph from e.t. archive, SH 004//c.
23 Brunel University Library.
24 Top: National Maritime Museum, photograph from e.t. archive, SH 004//c.
24 Bottom: Mystic Seaport Museum, 88-1-32.
25 Top: Anonymous 19th century view of *Great Eastern*. Sotheby's Picture Library. 850605/151.
25 Bottom left: Victoria and Albert Museum, photograph from e.t. archive, N-17/c.

25 Bottom middle: National Maritime Museum, B 1699.
25 Bottom right: National Maritime Museum, P 785.
26 Top: McCord Museum of Canadian History, Notman Photographic Archives, 7566-view.
26 Middle: McCord Museum of Canadian History, Notman Photographic Archives, view 7564-view.
26 Bottom: National Maritime Museum, P 10570.
26-27 *Splicing the Transatlantic Cable* by Robert Dudley. Private Collection, photograph from Bridgeman Art Library, 75458.
27 Top: The Mariners' Museum, PB 19959.
27 Bottom: The Mariners' Museum, PB 17220.
28 Top: The Mariners' Museum, PB 19085.
28 Bottom: The Mariners' Museum, PB 14058.
29 *Wreck of the Arctic.* The Mariners' Museum, LP 2327.
30 Eric Sauder Collection.
31 Top: Eric Sauder Collection.
31 Middle: Eric Sauder Collection.
31 Bottom: Eric Sauder Collection.
32 Top: Ken Schultz Collection.
32 Bottom: Mary Evans Picture Library.
33 Top left: Titanic Historical Society.
33 Bottom left: Popperfoto.
33 Right: Arnold Kludas Collection.
34 Left: Deutsches Schiffahrtsmuseum.
34 Upper right: Byron Collection, Museum of the City of New York.
34 Lower right: Byron Collection, Museum of the City of New York, 93.1.1.12492.
34 Bottom: Deutsches Schiffahrtsmuseum.
35 Top: The Mariners' Museum, PB 12388.
35 Bottom: Brown Brothers.
36 All: Arnold Kludas Collection.
37 Arnold Kludas Collection.

Chapter Two

38-39 Painting by Ken Marschall.
40-41: National Maritime Museum, Eric Sauder Collection.
40 Left: Eric Sauder Collection.
40 Right: Eric Sauder Collection.

42 Top: Eric Sauder Collection.
Middle: Brown Brothers.
Bottom: Brown Brothers.
43 Top: National Maritime Museum, photograph from e.t. archive, TR021-D.
43 Middle: Eric Sauder Collection.
43 Bottom: Eric Sauder Collection.
44 Top left: Eric Sauder Collection.
44 Middle left: Eric Sauder Collection.
44 Bottom left: The Mariners' Museum PB 25255.
44 Right: Eric Sauder Collection.
45 Top: Eric Sauder Collection.
45 Bottom: Eric Sauder Collection.
46: National Maritime Museum, N 22295.
46-47: Painting by Ken Marschall.
48 Top: Brown Brothers.
48 Middle: Eric Sauder Collection.
48 Bottom: Eric Sauder Collection.
49 Eric Sauder Collection.
50 Top: Eric Sauder Collection.
50 Bottom: The Mariners' Museum, PB 13552.
51 Top: Brown Brothers.
51 Bottom: Eric Sauder Collection.
52-53 Brown Brothers.
54-55 Painting by Ken Marschall.
55 Left: Eric Sauder Collection.
55 Right: Brown Brothers.
56-57 Painting by Ken Marschall.
57 Brown Brothers.
58-59 Painting by Ken Marschall.
59 Brown Brothers.
60 The Mariners' Museum, PB 16349.
61 Mary Evans Picture Library.
62-63 Painting by Ken Marschall.
63 Left: Eric Sauder Collection.
63 Top right: Jonathan Blair © National Geographic Society.
63 Bottom right: Photograph by Gary Gentile.
64-65 Painting by Ken Marschall.
64 Left: Jonathan Blair © National Geographic Society.
64 Middle: Jonathan Blair © National Geographic Society.
64 Right: Photograph by Gary Gentile.
65 Top: Jonathan Blair © National Geographic Society.
65 Bottom: Photograph by Gary Gentile.
66 Left: Courtesy of Odyssey Corporation.
66 Right: Jonathan Blair © National Geographic Society.
66-67 Painting by Ken Marschall.

67 Left: Photograph by Gary Gentile.
67 Right: Jonathan Blair © National Geographic Society.

Chapter Three

68-69 Painting by Ken Marschall.
70 Top: Ken Marschall Collection.
70 Bottom: Ken Marschall Collection.
71 The Mariners' Museum, PB 12869.
72-73 Brown Brothers.
73 Inset: Brown Brothers.
74 Top: Illustrated London News.
74 Bottom: Ulster Folk and Transport Museum.
75 Library of Congress, Ken Marschall Collection.
76 Left: Ken Marschall Collection.
76 Right: Ken Marschall Collection.
77 Top: Ken Marschall Collection.
77 Middle: Ken Marschall Collection.
77 Bottom: Ulster Folk and Transport Museum, Simon Mills Collection.
78 Top: Ken Marschall Collection.
78 Bottom: Ken Marschall Collection.
79 Top: Museum of the City of New York, Ken Marschall Collection.
79 Bottom left: Ken Marschall Collection.
79 Bottom right: Ken Marschall Collection.
80-81 Painting by Ken Marschall.
81 Southampton City Museum, Ken Marschall Collection.
82 Top: National Maritime Museum, N7684, Simon Mills Collection.
82 Bottom: National Maritime Museum, N7685, Simon Mills Collection.
83 Simon Mills Collection.
84 Father Browne S.J. Collection.
84-85 Painting by Ken Marschall, from the Dennis R. Kromm Collection.
86-87 Painting by Ken Marschall.
88-89 Painting by Ken Marschall.
90 Top: University of Pennsylvania Archives.
90 Bottom: Brown Brothers.
90-91 Painting by Ken Marschall.
92 Top: Brown Brothers.
92 Left: Brown Brothers.
92 Right: Brown Brothers.
93 Top left: Brown Brothers.
93 Bottom left: Brown Brothers.
93 Right: The Mariners' Museum.
94-95: Painting by Ken Marschall.

95 Top: Painting by Ken Marschall.
95 Bottom left: Woods Hole Oceanographic Institute.
95 Bottom right: Woods Hole Oceanographic Institute, Ken Marschall Collection.
96 Top: Woods Hole Oceanographic Institute.
96 Bottom left: Painting by Ken Marschall.
96 Bottom right: Painting by Ken Marschall.
96-97 Painting by Ken Marschall.
98 Top: Woods Hole Oceanographic Institute.
98 Middle left: Woods Hole Oceanographic Institute.
98 Middle right: Woods Hole Oceanographic Institute.
98 Bottom: Painting by Ken Marschall.
98-99 Painting by Ken Marschall.
100 Top: Southampton City Museum, Ken Marschall Collection.
100 Bottom: Ulster Folk and Transport Museum, Simon Mills Collection.
101 Left: Ken Marschall Collection.
101 Right: Deutsches Schiffahrtsmuseum.
102-103 Maritime Museum of the Atlantic, Ken Marschall Collection.
102 Bottom left: National Maritime Museum, Ken Marschall Collection.
102 Bottom middle: Ken Marschall Collection.
102 Bottom right: Ken Marschall Collection.
103 Ken Marschall Collection.
104 Left: Photograph by Peter Christopher.
104 Right top: Byron Collection, Museum of the City of New York, Ken Marschall Collection.
104 Right bottom: Photograph by Peter Christopher.
105 Top left: Photograph by Peter Christopher.
105 Middle upper: Harland and Wolff, Ken Marschall Collection.
105 Middle lower: Harland and Wolff, Ken Marschall Collection.
105 Top right: Photograph by Peter Christopher.
105 Bottom: Photograph by Peter Christopher.

106 Top: Alan Hustak Collection.
106 Bottom: UPI/Corbis-Bettmann, U13684 INP.
107 Top: Mark Reynolds Collection.
107 Bottom: Mark Reynolds Collection.
108 Artwork by Jack McMaster.
109 *Collier's* Magazine, Mark Reynolds Collection.
110 Left: UPI/Corbis-Bettmann, U13776INP.
110 Right: UPI/Corbis-Bettmann, U13798 INP.
111 Top: UPI/Corbis-Bettmann, U13783 INP.
111 Bottom left: UPI/Corbis-Bettmann, U13784 INP.
111 Bottom right: UPI/Corbis-Bettmann, U15192 INP.
112 Top: Photograph by Gary Gentile.
112 Bottom left: Photograph by Gary Gentile.
112 Bottom right: Photograph by Gary Gentile.
112-113: Painting by Ken Marschall.
114 Left: Photograph by Gary Gentile.
114 Top: Photograph by Philippe Beaudry.
114 Middle: Philippe Beaudry Collection.
114 Bottom: Photograph by Philippe Beaudry.
115 Photograph by Gary Gentile.

Chapter Four

116-117 Painting by Ken Marschall.
118-119 Imperial War Museum, Q73422, Simon Mills Collection.
118 Left: Karen Kamuda Collection.
118 Right: Karen Kamuda Collection.
120 Top: Ken Marschall Collection.
120 Left: Ulster Folk and Transport Museum, H2150A, Simon Mills Collection.
120 Lower left: Karen Kamuda Collection.
120 Right: Ulster Folk and Transport Museum, H2153, Simon Mills Collection.
121 Titanic Historical Society.
122 Top: Simon Mills Collection.
122 Bottom left: Simon Mills Collection.
122 Bottom middle: Simon Mills Collection.
122 Bottom right: Simon Mills Collection.
123 Simon Mills Collection.
124 Top: Ken Marschall Collection.
124 Middle: Simon Mills Collection.
124 Bottom: Simon Mills Collection.
125 Simon Mills Collection.
126 Painting by Ken Marschall.
127 Simon Mills Collection.

128 Top: Imperial War Museum, Q13657, Simon Mills Collection.
128 Bottom: Imperial War Museum, Simon Mills Collection.
129 Simon Mills Collection.
130 Artwork by Jack McMaster.
131 All: Artwork by Jack McMaster.
132 All: National Maritime Museum, Simon Mills Collection.
133 Simon Mills Collection.
134-135 Imperial War Museum, Simon Mills Collection.
136 Top: Photograph by Ken Marschall, Eric Sauder Collection.
136 Bottom: Courtesy of Odyssey Corporation.
136-137 Courtesy of Odyssey Corporation.
138 Left: Photograph by Ken Marschall.
138 Middle: Ken Marschall Collection.
138 Right: Photograph by Ken Marschall.
139 Painting by Ken Marschall.
140 Left: Titanic Historical Society.
140 Top right: Photograph by Ken Marschall.
140 Bottom right: Photograph by Ken Marschall.
141 Top: Photograph by Ken Marschall.
141 Bottom left: Photograph by Ken Marschall.
141 Bottom right: Photograph by Ken Marschall.
142-143 Photograph by Ken Marschall.
143 Top left: Ulster Folk and Transport Museum, Simon Mills Collection.
143 Bottom left: Ulster Folk and Transport Museum, courtesy of Titanic Historical Society.
143 Right: Photograph by Ken Marschall.

Chapter Five

144-145 Painting by Ken Marschall.
146 Top: Eric Sauder Collection.
146 Bottom: Eric Sauder Collection.
147 Top: Byron Collection, Museum of the City of New York.
147 Bottom left: Eric Sauder Collection.
147 Bottom right: Eric Sauder Collection.
148 Mary Evans Picture Library.
149 Top: The Mariners' Museum, PB-12314.
149 Bottom: Byron Collection, Museum of the City of New York, 93.1.1.11741.
150 Stanley Lehrer Collection.
151 Stanley Lehrer Collection.
152 John Provan Collection.

152-153 Deutsches Schiffarhtsmuseum.
154 Top: The Mariners' Museum, PB 31101.
154 Bottom left: Deutsches Schiffarhtsmuseum.
154 Bottom middle: Deutsches Schiffarhtsmuseum.
154 Bottom right: Deutsches Schiffarhtsmuseum.
155 Top: The Mariners' Museum, PB 27602.
155 Middle: Deutsches Schiffarhtsmuseum.
155 Bottom: Deutsches Schiffarhtsmuseum.
155 Right: Mary Evans Picture Library.
156 Top: Eric Sauder Collection.
156 Bottom: Eric Sauder Collection.
157 Mary Evans Picture Library.
158 Top: Carl House Collection.
158 Bottom: Mary Evans Picture Library.
159 Top: Stanley Lehrer Collection.
159 Bottom left: Byron Collection, Museum of the City of New York.
159 Bottom right: Carl House Collection.
160 Left: Carl House Collection.
160 Top right: Carl House Collection.
160 Bottom right: Carl House Collection.
161 Mary Evans Picture Library.
162 Top: Byron Collection, Museum of the City of New York, 93.1.1.11843.
162 Bottom: Stanley Lehrer Collection.
163 Byron Collection, Museum of the City of New York.
164 Top: Carl House Collection.
164 Bottom left: Stanley Lehrer Collection.
164 Bottom right: Carl House Collection.
165 Bottom: Eric Sauder Collection.
165 Top: Carl House Collection.
166 The Mariners' Museum, PB 262722.
166-167 Carl House Collection.
168 Byron Collection, Museum of the City of New York.
169 Brown Brothers.
170-171 Brown Brothers.
172 Eric Sauder Collection.
173 Left: Mary Evans Picture Library.
173 Top right: Eric Sauder Collection.
173 Middle right: Eric Sauder Collection.
173 Bottom right: Eric Sauder Collection.
174 Mary Evans Picture Library.
175 Top: Eric Sauder Collection.

175 Bottom: Eric Sauder Collection.
176-177 Painting by Ken Marschall, from the Eric Sauder Collection.
178 Brown Brothers.
179 Mary Evans Picture Library.
180 UPI/Corbis-Bettmann, UPI 944684 INP.
181 Left top: Carl House Collection.
181 Left bottom: Carl House Collection.
181 Right top: Corbis-Bettmann, U637149A.
181 Right bottom: Carl House Collection.
182-183 UPI/Corbis-Bettmann, UPI 944683.
183 Carl House Collection.
184 UPI/Corbis-Bettmann, UPI 944848 INP.
184 Inset: Stanley Lehrer Collection.
185 All: Artwork by Jack McMaster.
186 Top left: Photograph courtesy of Christie's Images.
186 Top right: Photograph courtesy of Christie's Images.
186 Middle: Byron Collection, Museum of the City of New York.
186 Bottom: Photograph courtesy of Christie's Images.
186 Right: Photograph courtesy of Christie's Images.
187 Left: Carl House Collection, photograph by Paul Kubek.
187 Inset: Carl House Collection
187 Top: Carl House Collection, photograph by Paul Kubek.
187 Middle left: Carl House Collection.
187 Middle right: Carl House Collection, photograph by Paul Kubek.
187 Bottom: Carl House Collection, photograph by Paul Kubek.

Chapter Six

188-189 Painting by Ken Marschall.
190 Eric Sauder Collection.
191 Top: Eric Sauder Collection.
191 Bottom: Eric Sauder Collection.
192 All: Eric Sauder Collection.
193 Top: Eric Sauder Collection.
193 Bottom: Mary Evans Picture Library.
194 Left: UPI/Corbis-Bettmann, 1002747.
194 Top right: Carl House Collection.
194 Middle right: Carl House Collection.
194 Bottom right: UPI/Corbis-Bettmann, 1199632 INP.
195 Left: Eric Sauder Collection.
195 Right: Corbis-Bettmann, C1200006.
196 Top: Photograph by Roland Herzil, Eric Sauder Collection.

196 Bottom: Photograph by Louis O. Gorman, Eric Sauder Collection.
197 Eric Sauder [T.H.S.] Collection.
199 UPI/Corbis-Bettmann, 1018292.
199 Middle: Photograph by Ed Scribner, Eric Sauder Collection.
199 Bottom: Photograph by Louis O. Gorman, Eric Sauder Collection.
200 Top: Titanic Historical Society.
200 Bottom: Titanic Historical Society.
201 Titanic Historical Society.
202 Artwork by Jack McMaster.
203 Top: UPI/Corbis-Bettmann, U-1319125-INP.
203 Bottom: Eric Sauder Collection.
204-205 Corbis-Bettmann, C1319043.
206 Top left: UPI/Corbis-Bettmann, U1319036 INP.
206 Middle left: The Mariners' Museum, photograph by Harry Trask, PB17136.
206 Bottom left: The Mariners' Museum, photograph by Harry Trask, PB17133.
206 Right: The Mariners' Museum, photograph by Harry Trask, PB17134.
207 Top left: The Mariners' Museum, photograph by Harry Trask, PB17137.
207 Middle left: The Mariners' Museum, photograph by Harry Trask, PB17135.
207 Bottom left: UPI/Corbis-Bettmann, UPI 1318995.
207 Right: Corbis-Bettmann, BHP 072616.
208 Painting by Ken Marschall, Eric Sauder Collection.
208-209 Painting by Ken Marschall, Eric Sauder Collection.
210 Photograph by Gary Gentile.
211 Top: Photograph by Brian Skerry.
211 Bottom: Photograph by Gary Gentile.
212 Top left: Eric Sauder Collection.
212 Top middle: Photograph by Gary Gentile.
212 Top right: Eric Sauder Collection.
212 Bottom: Photograph by Brian Skerry.
213 Left top: Eric Sauder Collection.
213 Left middle: Photograph by Gary Gentile.
213 Left bottom: Titanic Historical Society.
213 Right: Photograph by Brian Skerry.

Epilogue

215 Canapress.
216 All: Columbus America Discovery Group.

Bibliography

Anderson, Roy. *White Star*. Prescot, England: T. Stephenson & Sons, Ltd. 1964.

Archbold, Rick, and Dana McCauley. *Last Dinner on the Titanic*. New York: Hyperion, 1997.

Ardman, Harvey. *Normandie: Her Life and Times*. New York: Franklin Watts, 1985.

Bailey, Thomas A., and Paul B. Ryan. *The Lusitania Disaster*. New York: The Free Press, 1975.

Ballard, Robert D., with Spencer Dunsmore. *Exploring the Lusitania*. New York: Warner Books, 1995.

Ballard, Robert D., with Rick Archbold. *The Discovery of the Titanic*. New York: Warner Books, 1987.

Beesley, Lawrence. *The Loss of the Titanic*. London: William Heinemann, 1912.

Biel, Steven. *Down with the Old Canoe: A Cultural History of the Titanic Disaster*. New York: W. W. Norton, 1996.

Bisset, Sir James. *Tramps and Ladies*. New York: Criterion Books, 1959.

Braynard, Frank O. *Classic Ocean Liners, Volume 1: Berengaria, Leviathan & Majestic*. Wellingborough, England: Patrick Stephens Limited, 1990.

_____. *A Picture History of the Normandie*. New York: Dover Publications, 1987.

Brinnin, John Malcolm. *The Sway of the Grand Saloon*. New York: Delacorte Press, 1971.

Brinnin, John Malcolm, and Kenneth Gaulin. *Grand Luxe*. New York: Henry Holt & Company, 1988.

Britten, Sir Edgar T. *A Million Ocean Miles*. Wellingborough, England: Patrick Stephens, 1989.

Cecil, Lamar. *Albert Ballin*. Princeton: Princeton University Press, 1967.

Croall, James. *Fourteen Minutes: The Last Voyage of the Empress of Ireland*. London: Michael Joseph, 1978.

Eaton, John P., and Charles A. Haas. *Titanic: Triumph and Tragedy*. New York: W.W. Norton & Company, 1986.

Galbraith, Russell. *Destiny's Daughter: The Tragedy of RMS Queen Elizabeth*. Edinburgh: Mainstream Publishing Company Ltd., 1988.

Gentile, Gary. *Andrea Doria: Dive to an Era*. Philadelphia: Gary Gentile Productions, 1989.

Gracie, Colonel Archibald. *The Truth About the Titanic*. New York: Mitchell Kennerley, 1913.

Grattidge, Harry. *Captain of the Queens*. New York: E. P. Dutton & Co., 1956.

Hayes, Sir Bertram. *Hull Down*. New York: The Macmillan Company, 1925.

Hoehling, A. A., and Mary Hoehling. *The Last Voyage of the Lusitania*. New York: Henry Holt & Company, 1956.

Hoffer, William. *Saved! The Story of the Andrea Doria— the Greatest Sea Rescue in History*. New York: Summit Books, 1979.

Hughes, Tom. *The Blue Riband of the Atlantic*. Cambridge: Patrick Stephens, 1973.

Huldermann, Bernhard. *Albert Ballin*, translated by W. J. Eggers. London: Cassell & Co., 1922.

Hyslop, Donald, Alastair Forsyth and Sheila Jemima. *Titanic Voices*. Southampton, England: Oral History, City Heritage, Southampton City Council, 1994.

Jordan, Humfrey. *Mauretania*. Wellingborough, England: Patrick Stephens Limited, 1988.

Lightoller, Commander Charles H. *Titanic and Other Ships*. London: Ivor Nicholson and Watson, 1935.

Lord, Walter. *The Good Years: From 1900 to the First World War*. New York: Harper, 1960.

_____. *The Night Lives On*. New York: William Morrow & Company, Inc. 1986.

_____. *The Illustrated A Night to Remember*. Holt, Rinehart & Winston, 1976.

_____. *A Night to Remember*. New York: Henry Holt & Company, 1955.

Lynch, Don. *Titanic: An Illustrated History*. New York: Hyperion, 1992.

Marcus, Geoffrey. *The Maiden Voyage*. London: George Allen & Unwin, Ltd., 1969.

Maxtone-Graham, John. *The Only Way to Cross*. New York: Macmillan Publishing Company, 1972.

_____. *Cunard: 150 Glorious Years*. Newton Abbot: David & Charles, 1989.

Miller, Bill. *Ocean Liners*. Wigston, England: Magna Books, 1990.

Mills, Simon. *HMHS Britannic: The Last Titan*. Market Drayton, England: Shipping Books Press, 1996.

_____. *RMS Olympic: The Old Reliable*. Blandford Forum, England: Waterfront Publications, 1993.

Moscow, Alvin. *Collision Course*. New York: Grosset & Dunlap, 1981.

Ocean Liners of the Past: The White Star Triple Screw Atlantic Liners Olympic and Titanic. Cambridge: Patrick Stephens, 1983.

Offrey, Charles. *Normandie: Queen of the Seas*. New York: Vendome Press, 1985.

Oldham, Wilton J. *The Ismay Line*. Liverpool: Charles Birchall & Sons, Ltd., 1961.

Potter, Neil, and Jack Frost. *The Queen Mary: Her Inception and History*. San Francisco: San Francisco Press, Inc., 1971.

Protasio, John. *To the Bottom of the Sea*. New York: Carol Publishing Group, 1990.

Roche, T. W. E. *Samuel Cunard and the North Atlantic*. London: Macdonald & Company Ltd., 1971.

Rostron, Sir Arthur H. *Home From the Sea*. New York: The Macmillan Company, 1931.

Sauder, Eric, and Ken Marschall, with Bill Sauder. *R.M.S. Lusitania: Triumph of the Edwardian Age*. Redondo Beach, Cal.: Trans-Atlantic Designs, 1991.

U.S. Senate, Subcommittee Hearings of the Committee on Commerce, 62nd Congress. *Titanic Disaster*. Washington, D.C.: Government Printing Office, 1912.

Wade, Wyn Craig. *The Titanic: End of a Dream*. New York: Rawson, Wade Publishers, Inc., 1979.

Wall, Robert. *Ocean Liners*. Seacaucus, New Jersey: Chartwell Books, Inc., 1977.

Warren, Mark D. *The Cunard Turbine-Driven Quadruple-Screw Atlantic Liner "Lusitania."* Wellingborough, England: Patrick Stephens, 1986.

Whale, Derek M. *The Liners of Liverpool*, parts 1-3. Merseyside, England: Countyvise Limited, 1986.

The White Star Triple Screw Atlantic Liners Olympic and Titanic. Cambridge, England: Patrick Stephens, 1983.

Wreck Commissioners' Court, Proceedings Before the Right Honourable Lord Mersey, on a Formal Investigation Ordered by the Board of Trade into the Loss of the SS "Titanic."

Newspapers and magazines

The Titanic Commutator, published by the Titanic Historical Society (P.O. Box 51053, Indian Orchard, Massachusetts 01151-0053, U.S.A.) is an invaluable resource, not only for material relating to the *Titanic* and her sisters but to passenger steamships throughout the great age of ocean travel.

Index

DESIGN AND ART DIRECTION: GORDON SIBLEY DESIGN INC.

EDITORIAL DIRECTOR: HUGH M. BREWSTER

PROJECT EDITOR: IAN R. COUTTS

COPY EDITOR: ALISON REID

EDITORIAL ASSISTANCE: SUSAN AIHOSHI

PRODUCTION DIRECTOR: SUSAN BARRABLE

PRODUCTION COORDINATOR: SANDRA L. HALL

ORIGINAL PAINTINGS: KEN MARSCHALL

MAPS AND DIAGRAMS: JACK MCMASTER

COLOR SEPARATION: COLOUR TECHNOLOGIES

PRINTING AND BINDING: SFERA/GARZANTI

LOST LINERS WAS PRODUCED BY
MADISON PRESS BOOKS,
WHICH IS UNDER THE DIRECTION OF
ALBERT E. CUMMINGS